T[illegible]
Sacred Parenting

Foreword by

Rev. Dr. John Wesley White
of the
Billy Graham Evangelical Association

The Art of Sacred Parenting

No Ordinary Moments

by

Dr. John S. Niles

Vital Lessons from the Father of 1000 Children

From the New White Knight Series:

A Better Way of Living

Foreword by

Rev. Dr. John Wesley White of the
Billy Graham Evangelical Association.

White Knight Books
Toronto, Canada

Published in 2006 by White Knight Books,
a division of Bill Belfontaine Ltd.
Suite 103, One Benvenuto Place, Toronto Ontario Canada M4V 2L1
T. 416-925-6458 F. 416-925-4165
e-mail whitekn@istar.ca • www.whiteknightbooks.ca

Distributions Services
White Knight Book Distribution Services Ltd.
c/o Georgetown Terminal Warehouses
34 Armstrong Avenue, Georgetown ON, L7G 4R9
Tel: 866-485-5556 Fax: 866-485-6665
e-mail: order@gtwcanada.com

Library and Archives Canada Cataloguing in Publication

Niles, John S., 1962-
The art of sacred parenting : no ordinary moments / John S. Niles.
Sequel to: How I became father to 1000 children.
ISBN 0-9736705-7-6
1. Child welfare—Canada. 2. Child abuse—Canada.
3. Children's rights—Canada. I. Title.
BX9883.N45A3 2006 362.7'0971 C2006-900364-5

Cover and text design: Karen (Petherick) Thomas,
Intuitive Design International Ltd.

Editing: Bill Belfontaine
Printed and Bound in Canada

DEDICATION

I dedicate this book to my wife Liane.

My life began when I met you. You are cotton candy, popcorn and candy apples. You are a day at the carnival and a night in front of a glowing fire. You are the amazing mother of our children, the love of my life and the one who still takes my breath away.

And to our five children Sarah, Alyssa, Nathanael, Aaron, and Tabitha. You are the best of us. Don't grow up too fast. But when you do, remember—You are loved!

And to the thousand and more children we have cared for and thousands of children who have yet to find a safe place to belong; may this be the year they become loved and fulfilled.

And finally, I dedicate this work to my Lord and Savior Jesus Christ.
To You be all glory, honor and praise.

CONTENTS

Your children are not your children

They are the sons and daughters of life's longing for itself

They come through you but not from you,

And though they are with you yet they belong not to you

You may give them your love but not your thoughts

For they have their own thoughts.

You may house their bodies not their souls.

For their souls dwell in the house of tomorrow,

which you cannot visit, not even in your dreams.

You may strive to be like them,

but seek not to make them like you.

For life goes not backward nor tarries with yesterday.

— • —

Kahil Gibran

FOREWORD

Dr John Wesley White

As Dr. Billy Graham's associate I have travelled the world preaching the Gospel. I have known hundreds of ministers and hundreds of thousands of people during this time and have only accepted a very few to be on my board of directors. Dr. John Niles is one of these who I was honored to have on my board of directors of Join the Family Ministries under the Billy Graham Evangelistic Association.

I first met Dr. Niles when he was vice chairman planning Mission Ontario with Billy Graham. I was impressed not only with his leadership ability—which is vast—but with his ability to communicate truth with relevant and penetrating accuracy. He is an exceptional preacher and communicator.

As I have come to know Dr. Niles over the years, I have been both humbled and inspired by his compassion for those who are in need. His love of the Gospel is evident throughout his life and work, as well as his skillful leadership and compassionate service. He has garnered not only the respect of his peers but also the respect of the Government of Canada receiving one of the *three* highest honors Canada gives to her citizens, the Governor General's Meritorious Service Medal, and being nominated for the two other highest honors that Canada gives to her citizens the Order of Ontario and the Order of Canada; which he will undoubtedly receive in the future.

Dr. Niles' first book, *"How I Became Father to 1000 Children and the Lessons Learned,"* was so impressive that I was again proud to be able to call him my friend and doubly honored to have him on my board.

His second book—*The Art of Sacred Parenting*—that I am privileged to write the foreword for it exemplifies his insightful ability to communicate significant truth in relevant and comprehensible ways.

It is more than a book about parenting. It is a book about life. It is a book that is meant to remind people that life is sacred and that it is our sacred responsibility to raise our children to be humane human beings.

We live in violent times where there are "wars and rumor of wars," where children are killing children, where guns are used to settle arguments and where gangs for some youth are replacing the family for that sense of security. We need a more humane world. Dr. Niles successfully instructs us, through the lessons he has learned from caring for hundreds of abused children, how to become more humane human beings not taking this life for granted but understanding that each moment we have is sacred and that there are, no ordinary moments.

There is no doubt you will benefit by reading this book—I have. Read it, enjoy it, and learn from it and then read it again.

Dr. John Wesley White (Oxon)
Toronto, Ontario, Canada

PREFACE

The Art of Sacred Parenting: Learning to Be Human

He who isn't busy being born is busy dying. ~ *Bob Dylan*

Parenting is a sacred trust. It is where the past and the future commune. As Kahil Gibran wrote, "Your children are not your children... You may house their bodies not their souls, for their souls dwell in the house of tomorrow..." Each parent holds the souls of their children in their hands. Each child is a gift from God entrusted to their parents for their well being, as well as for their learning and becoming human beings.

The primary virtues and values that lead to experiencing the sacredness of life—and having the blessed life—are meant to be passed down from parents to children. This sacred privilege of parents is sometimes lost on various children due to their parent's lack of awareness, insight, ability or willingness to bless their children with this knowledge. Instead of the children experiencing life's sanctity they encounter life's brutality.

It is the parent's joyful duty and profound responsibility to help their children develop the virtues and values necessary to become fully realized human beings. Plato described virtue as "a kind of health, beauty and habit of the soul." Albert Einstein proposed, "Only morality in action gives beauty and dignity to life." When this is grasped we discover to our delight that there are *no ordinary moments.*

Life is filled with moments—just moments in time. However,

when we take the time to look at them, we discover that there are *no ordinary moments*.

I was able to catch a glimpse of this concept one December evening when my daughter Tabitha had been five years old at the time and was excited to take Star, a little baby girl who came to us at birth and had been with us nearly a year, to see Santa. She had found two pair of toy reindeer antlers in with the decorations and had decided that they were going to be dressed like reindeer for Santa. Tabitha had slipped into my bedroom, without my wife noticing and took my wife Liane's red lipstick and colored her nose bright red and put the antlers on her head and on baby Star's head as well.

When I arrived home from work, I was greeted at the door by the two of them. Tabitha clasped Star's hand and said, with the determination that only a five year old could have that was on a mission to introduce her new little foster sister to Santa, "Mommy says that *you* are taking us to see Santa today."

"Am I?" I asked.

"Yes."

"Well, who are you?"

"Daddy, you know who I am. I'm Rudolph the Red Nose Reindeer."

"And is this Star the reindeer?" I said.

"No," said Tabitha, "There is no Star the reindeer. Daddy, don't you know anything? This is Olive."

"Olive?" I said, quite confused.

"Yes, you know, like the song. Then she began in a sweet little sing-song voice, "Olive the other reindeer used to laugh and call him names...You know Olive"

"How could I have forgotten?" I said.

I haven't since. She was nearly four when she left us to be adopted. We had three and a half years filled with far from ordinary moments. And it has been three years since Star was adopted and each year as I take out the decorations from beneath the stairs and begin to trim the tree I find myself fumbling through the boxes of ornaments and Christmas knick knacks until I find the reindeer ears, put them on my head and think again of Rudolph and Olive—the other reindeer.

Christmas is a time of past memories and cherished moments. It is a time of new beginnings, and future memories waiting to be born. But for me it will always be one that includes Rudolph and Olive—the other reindeer; because in the sweetness of that moment remembered is all the warmth of the season, and the gracefulness and gentleness of child-like hopes and sugar-plum dreams that makes Christmas—Christmas. Just a moment in time, but it was *no ordinary moment.*

There are no ordinary moments in life when we see our parenting as sacred. Yet, perhaps as a parent, you feel both "drawn and quartered" by life—pulled in so many different directions you fear that you are going to come apart—and also strangely drawn to a deeper way of life, one that longs to catch those special, yet sacred moments, that I spoke of with Rudolph and Olive. If that is the case then read on. For contained within this book are the virtues and values, lessons and principles that make for a life filled with *no ordinary moments.*

CAN VIRTUE BE LEARNED?

Can virtue be learned? I believe it can. The reason that I am so sure that it can be learned is that I have been attempting to learn the profoundly important but simple virtues all my life and pass them on to my children and others. The virtues that are spoken about in this book may have been, in the past, dismissed as passé within our culture, but no longer. As we see the world around us crumble into an abyss of violence and inhumanity and brutality, we all comprehend the need to return to the virtues that draw us to an elevated way of living and being.

Virtues can be found in all of the world's sacred literature. For thousands of years people have used them as the foundational principles of their lives. They are considered the character traits of the human spirit, something universal to every culture. Each society has their own list of virtues. And each culture may differ about which virtue is more important than others but all consider them to be essential to human well-being and happiness.

Life is meant to be more than seeking more business, more money, more work, or sales, but rather becoming more human, and that way leaving behind a more humane world. The only way to have a good society is to have a good individual.

Confucius said:

If there is harmony in the heart, there will be
harmony in the family.
If there is harmony in the family there will be
harmony in the nation.
If there is harmony in the nation, there will be
harmony in the world.

There is disharmony on a substantial scale in our world. And that is because there is disharmony is our hearts. I live with the effects of this disharmony on a daily basis. I see it each time we receive a little baby in our home at 3 a.m. with broken bones and cigarette burns covering its body. I see it each time I meet the parents of these shattered children, only to see broken human beings who themselves never received the knowledge that they were a gift from God and that they had been given a sacred trust as parents of their little ones.

I had always believed in the value of the virtues that you will find in this book. However, it was only after I began caring for over 1000 heroin and crack addicted babies and abandoned abused infants and toddlers in our own home over the last 20 years that I began to esteem these virtues in a more significant way. Though the virtues remained the same, the value of these virtues increased in my eyes because of the impact they had on my life and the lives of these children as I cared for these fragile and fractured little human beings. I learned the depth and breadth of their importance one child at a time.

We acquired the word virtue from the Greeks word *arête* which means "excellences" and was translated by the Romans as *virtus.* "Taken in its widest sense virtue means the excellence of perfection of a thing, just as vice, its contrary, denotes a defect or absence of perfection due to a thing…"[1]

LEARNING TO BE HUMAN

Why are virtues so important? It is because it is through them that we learn to be human. These virtues are the spiritual muscles that grow and help us to develop into the people we were created to be. The virtues of courage, kindness, moderation, compassion, forgiveness, generosity, mercy, justice, faith, hope and love; all are vitally important to being and becoming human. They are the reason that there are in life *no ordinary moments.*

Why is it that it is so easy to be inhuman? I am haunted by this question. Each time I gather a shattered child in my arms, look into her tear-filled eyes, tend her broken bones, and ravaged skin I am left profoundly disturbed by the reality of this world. When I wrote my first book, *How I Became Father to 1000 Children and the Lessons Learned,* implicit within the title was that question that has disturbed me for more than twenty years.

Why are people so inhumane? Why can't human beings just be humane? Why is it that a child, who wants nothing more than to be loved and held and fed, will instead be abused, battered and discarded? For that matter, why do we think we can do that with any person at any age? Why do we think that we can treat each other with such brutality and not betray who we are at the core of our being? Can we really call ourselves human if we are not humane?

What does it mean to be human? Certainly, we are human by birth, but that does not make us humane by nature. We are given the greatest gift at birth. That gift is life. Yet, too often we reach the end of our life never having fully lived. Bob Dylan echoed this fear when he stated that the greatest tragedy in life is that most human beings "died before they were fully born."

Learning to be human is what children are all designed to do. It is encoded on their genes. From the moment a child is born they set out instinctively to learn about everything. They are sponges that soak up life. They are driven and determined to learn. Learning to be human is what children do; but somewhere along the way some of us begin to loose our focus and as adults we fail to continue to learn those lessons and we become embittered and hard and bored. We fail to experience life with the same joy and excitement that we did as a child, when everything was new and an adventure in life.

Wordsworth speaks to this,

Our birth is but a sleep and a forgetting,
The soul that raises with us its life star
Has else where its setting and cometh from afar,
Not in entire forgetfulness and not in utter nakedness
But trailing clouds of glory do we come from God

Who is our home, Heaven lays about us in our infancy...
The prison door closes on a growing boy...

Wordsworth was right. As we draw nearer to being adults, we grow less enamored with learning, and becoming, and turn away to involve ourselves in doing and acquiring.

Elie Wiesel tells us of a rabbi who has said that when we die and go to meet our Creator the question asked of us will not be why you did not become a powerful leader, or a famous person, or a multi-millionaire but simply why you did not become *you,* the fully realized human being that only you had the potential of being.

Keats has written that "This world is a vale of soul making." And he is right. In life we are matured and molded in the midst of all that happens to us. And yet, many choose to give up because things don't go just right. Life can make us, or break us. It really depends on how we face life's adversity. That was a lesson I learned from many of the children we have cared for over the last 20 years.

If you read my first book you already know that I have learned a great deal from those thousand, abandoned, abused, infants and toddlers. I have seen the most viciously abused children respond to loving, trusting acceptance. I have seen children overcome what seemed insurmountable odds. And I have been left continually in awe of their dogged determination to overcome.

This world is "a vale of soul making." It is the place where we learn to be human if we are open to the lessons that life offers us. Each parent involves themselves by intentionally assisting their children in the process of learning to be human and in doing so they take on their true vocation as a sacred parent and discover that there are *no ordinary moments.*

SECTION I

The Principal Lessons

courage is fear
that has said its prayers

— • —

Karl Barth

Whenever parents are asked what they want their children to be when they grow up, without exception parents in the western world say, "I want my daughter to be happy." "I want my son to be happy." Americans have enshrined the "pursuit of happiness" in their Constitution legally, and Canadians have enshrined it in our constitution psychologically.

The pursuit of happiness has always been a way of life across the world. However, what most people differ on is the definition of happiness. Plato, Socrates, Augustine, Aquinas and many other classical and Christian thinkers have spent time writing and thinking about what makes a life happy. The Beatitudes of Jesus as recorded in St. Matthew's account of the Sermon on the Mount has also to do with happiness. The word beatitude in Greek means blessed or happy. However, none of these thinkers would say that happiness is found only in gratifying the physical wants and needs.

Today, however, we are seeing the result of those who have lived by the view of self-gratification. The often heard joke in the business world is, "He who dies with the most toys wins." Wins what? The scandals of the Enrons, Nortels and Arthur Andersons seemed to have shown the emptiness of the mindset of happiness found only in self-gratification and greed.

Parents have a sacred responsibility to their child and to the world. When a parent truly grasps this (and I must admit that I have only done so *consciously* in the last few years) they come to understand they have been given an opportunity to change the world.

No matter how often we tell our children, "You can be an thing you want to be. You could even be Prime Minister or President," none of us knows if our child will achieve any greatness or do any good. However, if we want them to be fully realized human beings, making their mark, in their unique way parents must play the crucial role in making that happen.

Nelson Mandela, Mother Teresa, Martin Luther King Jr. were all given the tools by their parents at a young age. If that were not true they would never have achieved what they did. That is what Sacred Parenting is all about. Taking seriously the role and responsibility of being a parent; it is to understand that the possibilities in each child are infinite and choosing to nurture those possibilities. When we do so we give our child the needed foundation, motivation and inspiration to become what God intended and created them to be.

Samuel Coleridge commented on happiness:

"But we were not made to find Happiness in the complete gratification of our bodily wants—the mind must enlarge its sphere of activity and progressive by nature, must never rest content. For this purpose our Almighty Parent hath given us Imagination that stimulates to the attainment of real excellence, by the contemplation of splendid possibilities, that still revivifies the dying motives within us and fixing our eyes on the glittering Summits that rise one above the other in alpine endlessness, still urges us up the ascent of being."[2]

Happiness then must rather be defined as a life well lived. A life well lived comes not from acquiring the most toys but by making the most of the gifts of life you have. If as parents we have happiness as the objective for our life and the life of our children then the means of attaining true happiness is found in living life properly.

Every great thinker and philosopher has pointed to the primary or "cardinal" virtues as the means of attaining a life worth living. St. Thomas Aquinas, who in the *Summa Theologica,* lists what he viewed were the primary or cardinal virtues as justice, prudence, temperance, and fortitude. I have sought to modernize the language to call them wisdom, justice, courage and self-discipline.

HABITS OF BEING

"Virtue", says Augustine, "is a good habit consonant with our nature." Saint Thomas said of virtue, *habitus operatives bonus,* "an operative habit essentially good".

My mother used to quote a little poem which speaks to this habit of being.

Sow a thought, reap an act
Sow an act, reap a habit
Sow a habit, reap a character
Sow a character, reap a destiny

There is an edge to this. It cuts both ways, just as there are virtues that can become habitual in a way that creates positive characteristics in a person and a productive destiny; so too, can there be vices which create negative characteristics in a person that can reap a destructive destiny.

Sacred Parenting is about assisting your children in forming the habits of a lifetime. This begins as a child is loved, encouraged, praised, rewarded, and consequenced for their actions. When you reward and reinforce the positive values and virtues and lovingly consequence and discipline the negative; you are preparing and nurturing the character of your child. You are helping them begin to grow into humane human beings. You are helping them understand that in life there are consequences—both positive and negative—to their actions. You are helping them make choices in life that will reap rich rewards in the future.

We live in a broken world which creates broken people. These broken people then give birth and raise broken children. I have spent the last 25 years helping and healing broken lives. In our work as an emergency home we have nurtured and loved, worked and watched as these fragile little human beings begin to heal physically, psychologically, emotionally and spiritually. I have watched them transform from being terrified of the unknown when they are brought into our home and after a few hours and days become overjoyed at being in a place where they are safe, loved and protected. I have watched as they move from being bitter and defensive to being sweet and loving. I have seen them despair of life and then begin to delight in it. We have helped them move from having no future to having a bright one. That is what Sacred Parenting is about. Whether this is done with your own children or with others; whether you are a parent, grandparent, teacher, foster parent, big brother, or big sister, mentor or teacher, Sacred Parenting is about changing the world one child at a time.

Augustine said, "The soul needs to follow something in order to give birth to virtue. This something is God, and if we follow Him, we shall live the good life."[3]

The primary or cardinal virtues when practiced and/or taught improve not only the present but the future. We have all heard it said, "Practice makes perfect." It is true for all of life.

My mother wanted me to learn piano. I took piano lessons for eight years and still only know "chopsticks" with my knuckles. Yet, I know of others who began at the same time who are now concert pianists. I didn't value, at that time, either the lessons or the instrument and so I learned nothing. I regret that now, because it would have made my work in the ministry so much easier and life so much sweeter if I had practiced and learned how to play the piano.

The same is true in life. Many people live lives filled with regret due to the fact that they never valued, learned or practiced life's vital virtues. It is the highest duty and responsibility of a parent to mold the character of a child. Children are shaped by their parents and home environments into being the people they become. Parents help to develop the way children perceive life and the way life is experienced by them. The early lessons in the home help the children make the right choices later in life that then makes life worth living.

Parents have the enormous task of giving their children the tools necessary to equip them to be better human beings which will in turn make the world more humane. Sacred Parenting involves raising children to not only be human beings but also humane beings. If the world is to be a better place, and children are to be free from violence and abuse, and society is to rest on a firm foundation, then parents need to comprehend that we have the sacred trust given us to raise our children as moral and spiritual beings. When we, as parents, provide reliable principles, unmistakable values, and unequivocal virtues to our children then the world becomes a safer and more humane place for them to live, grow and become and they too begin to experience that there are in life *no ordinary moments.*

The character development of a child begins at birth. The shaping of the heart and mind of a child toward the good is the life's work of parent who see what they are doing as a sacred trust. The constructive development of the child's character occurs as these virtues are lovingly nurtured in the life of a child.

Within this book you will find the reliable principles, unmistakable values, and unequivocal virtues needed for you to raise your child into becoming a humane human being and to put into practice the principles of Sacred Parenting and humane living.

1

Life Is A Gift—Accept It

How would you reply if I said, "Today you are going to get what you deserve." There is an edge to it, isn't there? You really never know if it is good or bad. The reality is there are consequences. Every good parent wants to teach their children the lesson of consequences. It is because that is how real life works and wisdom is gained. Every parent knows that if a child is to experience the richness of life they must understand the rules of life. They must grasp the wisdom lessons that are built into the very fabric of life.

T. S. Eliot stated, "Where is the wisdom we have lost in knowledge and where is the knowledge we have lost in information." We live in an information age. With the creation of the internet we have more information on more subjects at our very fingertips than at any other time in history. However, does the acquisition of information and knowledge make us wise? I don't think so. I know this because of the work I do with children. I am continually shocked at the ignorance of judges who return children home to an abusive life-threatening situation simply because these adults gave birth to the child. It is as if just because you give birth you automatically know what you are doing and care about knowing what is necessary to care for the child. In most cases people do care. They have support from family and seek knowledge from friends and classes and books. But in the cases where the parents don't care to learn but only care about getting their "property" back, I often wonder if the judges who decide to send the child home again understand that the child's life is in danger. I want to cry out, "What are you THINKING!"

I could give hundreds of stories where this has happened, however, let me tell just one. She came to us at birth. She was born to a mother on crack who tested positive every time she was required by the court to be tested during the nine months that Betty was in our care. She rarely came to the supervised visits to see Betty and when she did was obviously high. Yet, the judge sent her home with her mother. We objected but to no avail. Our pleas fell on deaf ears. We hoped that she would not be found dead, but feared she would be. By some miracle a month later she was found alone in a filthy crack house malnourished but alive. She was taken into care again. However, she was not allowed to be placed with us because we already had two babies under two years old at the time. Her place was taken by another needy child. As a result, she was placed elsewhere. I have often wondered if those judges ever learned that their actions and decisions have such consequences.

Knowledge and information without wisdom is useless. However, acquiring wisdom is vital to life. And it is the responsibility of every loving parent to nurture its growth in their child so that they aspire to become a humane human being.

Teaching these lessons can be frustrating. George Washington's mother was once asked how she raised such a remarkable son. "I taught him to obey," she answered. This is not always easy. Wisdom lessons begin simply. They begin by teaching the simple lessons to start with. It begins by teaching children manners. Saying "Please" and "Thank You" and "I'm Sorry". It involves lessons like "Keep your hands to yourself." "Look both ways before crossing the road." "Chew with your mouth closed." "Don't stick raisins up your nose." "Don't hide peas in your pockets." "Don't go to the bathroom in the neighbor's yard even if their dog goes in ours." "Don't chew gum that's already been chewed, and you found under a chair." "Don't close the car door when Daddy's hand is on the door." "Don't flush mummy's things down the toilet." "Don't cut your own hair." *Don't* cut your sisters hair." Why? Not just because I said so, but because there are consequences.

EVERYTHING HAS A CONSEQUENCE

The mistake that most of us, with children, have made is to think that the wise and loving thing to do for our child—when they do something wrong or get into trouble—is to save the child from experiencing the consequence. The fact is the best thing we can do for our children is to let them learn very early that there are natural and logical consequences to every action. To do so will save them from a great deal of grief and sorrow later in life. Most of the early consequences, are not life threatening. However, later on they might be and the consequence dramatically life changing.

I still remember when I stole a pack of Juicy Fruit Gum from the local grocers. I was six and started chewing it on the way home in the car with my parents. That was my second mistake. My mother took me into the house and I told her I took the gum, I was disciplined and then marched—and I mean marched we were a military family—to the local store. I again confessed and paid for the gum out of my piggy bank. I never forgot that lesson—and never stole again.

Years ago parents taught these lessons through poems and stories. One of the poems my mother used often was found in Aesop's fables. She would bring the book of fables to the table and begin to read from *The Flies and the Honey Pot.* After which she asked if I understood what the poem was about and expected me to explain it and apply it to my situation.

The Flies and the Honey Pot

A jar of honey chanced to spill
Its contents on the windowsill
In many a viscous pool and rill.

The flies, attracted by the sweet,
Began so greedily to eat,
They smeared their fragile wings and feet.
With many a twitch and pull in vain
They gasped to get away again,
And died in aromatic pain

Moral
O foolish creatures that destroy
Themselves for transitory joy

There are consequences to actions. They may not always be immediate. However, there are always consequences whether they are internal or external. And Sacred Parenting is about teaching this lesson and others to our children.

Robertson Davies, the great Canadian novelist describes this as the moral reality. He said when describing his writing, "I am a type of writer that one could call a moralist. A moralist is one who looks at human conduct with as clear an eye as he can manage ... and observes that quite often people reap what they have sown. For God is not mocked."

Even if there is no external consequence to a bad or self-defeating behavior there is an internal one. This is a lesson that children need to understand. We need, for our children's emotional, spiritual and ethical well-being, to understand that there is always a consequence. The internal consequence is that they are changed because of the behavior. I often quote from a children's poem.

There was a crooked man
who walked a crooked mile
He found a crooked sixpence
upon a crooked stile.
He bought a crooked cat which
caught a crooked mouse,
And they all lived together in
a little crooked house

Why was the man's world crooked? It was crooked because he was. He was a crook and his crookedness twisted his whole world out of shape.

William James tells us that we may say of what we have done, "It won't count this time." But it does count. It is registered deep within us, shaping our personality, influencing us at levels of which we are not aware, and finally, if repeated often enough, making us what we are—for good or ill.

Do you remember how in the *Lion in Winter* King Henry loved Eleanor his Queen? In their youth they came together with passion and delight and loved with joy. Later he keeps her locked up in the Tower and allows her out for a Christmas visit. And even then they come with drawn knives to cut and wound each other. In a reflective moment, one asks the other, "How, from where we were, did we get to where we are?" And the other replies," "A little bit at a time." It's true. To deny it is to deny truth.

There was a news report a few years ago about a women in a little town in Germany. She had been raised with the belief that this little town had nothing to do with Nazism. Rather, it spoke out against it and worked against it during Hitler's years in power.

In her last year of high school she decided to do a project about this. They wanted to promote and praise the people for this. The problem was she found it to be a brazen lie. A few years later she continued her research and found that they fully backed Hitler. That is what she wrote in the paper. As a result she was run out of town and her husband divorced her. She now lives somewhere in the United States. Is it any wonder that White Supremacy is on the rise in Germany and violence on the increase there? They planted that seed and have watered it with denial, rather then uprooting it with truth.

WHAT ARE YOU AFTER?

Every person who takes seriously their sacred responsibility as a parent has dealt with this question. It determines how you live your life and how your child will in turn learn from you how to live theirs.

In 1985, Ivan Boesky addressed a group of business students. He told them, "Greed is all right by me. I think greed is healthy. You can be greedy and still feel good about yourself." He said it so well that he got a standing ovation from the students. Not long after, he received a jail sentence and was fined $100,000,000. Is there good greed? I don't know of any.

The Broadway play *Serious Money* and the film *Wall Street* were loosely based on his life. An astute reviewer said, "It was a portrayal of temptation, a scandal about junk bonds, and the savings and loan disaster driven by selfish ambition."

What is it that you are after? What is it that you are sowing into the soil of your life? Is it smothering you, choking off the life that is in you? Is what you are doing slowly sapping you of strength; stealing from your dignity. If it is you can be sure that it will happen in your children as well.

The Mossad, Israel's secret service, tells us that they can get nearly any male by one or some combination of three things, power, women, or money. One of the earliest documents written was found and it was written by a Roman centurion, "In this life you can either have love or power, but you can't have both."

What is it that you are seeking? I know many people who are after the approval of others. And very often they will do anything to get it; even things that they would never do otherwise.

There are always consequences to our choices. A fellow-journalist of Malcolm Muggeridge said to him in an open air cafe in Vienna, "Malcolm, sometimes I wonder if I am licking the right boots." Why would anyone want to lick another's boots? Yet, people do it all the time. They settle for power, and so must expect never to have love for it is hard to have both. Or they want justice and not mercy. If that is the case then they had better not make a mistake. Others accept the belief that life is a rat race. In doing so they don't realize they must not if they desire a life of dignity. Still others settle for security. And therefore may have to forgo ecstasy. For life is moral and we do reap what we sow, so whatever you chose has its own cost. Sacred Parenting means teaching such a lesson.

RIGHT LIVING

I have so often found that people don't know what they are after. They just fill their lives with things hoping that they can have it all, and that somehow something they have brought into their life will bring meaning and fulfillment, often leaving no room for those things that are truly important to them. They leave out the thing that brings meaning and fulfillment, and so they live diminished lives—lives that rarely bloom or blossom, because they have been smothered by the fog and deafened by the noise of life. In doing so, they teach their children to do the same. The famous adage applies, "The apple never falls far from the tree." If we want the best for our children, we must seek the best for ourselves.

Children Learn What They Live

If a Child lives with criticism, He learns to condemn.
If a child lives with hostility, she learns to fight.
If a child lives with ridicule, he learns to be shy.
If a child lives with shame, she learns to be guilty.
If a child lives with tolerance, he learns to be patient.
If a child lives with encouragement, she learns confidence.
If a child lives with praise, he learns to appreciate.
If a child lives with fairness, she learns justice.
If a child lives with security, he learns to have faith.
If a child lives with approval, she learns to like herself.
If a child lives with acceptance and friendship,
he learns to find love in the world.

Anon.

Stephen Covey, when addressing a conference on time management, displayed a clear glass jar then placed three large rocks in it. He asked the question; "Can I get anymore in the jar?" The answer was no, for they thought he meant more large rocks. Then he put in a large amount of pebbles and asked the same question. People were sure this time nothing more could get in. So Covey took out sand, and poured that in. He then asked the same question. "Can anything more fit in?" This time the audience had finally caught on and said yes. He pulled out a jar of water and poured that in. He asked what this illustrated.

One man stood and said, "I think it means that if I look, I can always find time to put more things into my life."

"Wrong! It illustrates," Covey said, "that if I hadn't put the three large rocks in first, I wouldn't have gotten them in."

So often we leave the important things out of our lives—real commitment to God, and our commitment to our wives or husbands, and children—and we fill our lives up with things that sap our energy and smother the flowering of our spirits and our children's spirits.

I recall a conversation I had with a friend who I often visited when he was dying. He said, "There is wonderful freedom in dying. No, I wouldn't wish it on anyone. But, as a believer in Jesus, I see things now in a way I didn't see before. I see more clearly now, what is really important. All those meetings I used to see as so important—they're dust; all those positions I held—they are refuse; all that prestige and importance—garbage. I see now with clarity of vision that I have never had before, that my faith in Jesus and my family and the legacy I am leaving is what are important. Take it from me, no dying man is ever going to say, I wish I had spent more time at the office. They are going to say, I wish, I spent more time getting to know God—if they fear death—or I wish I spent more time with my family. I wish I spent more time doing what really mattered and making a difference, leaving my mark in some way. Never neglect your faith or your family, John."

Dag Hammorjold once said, "You can't plant a garden and reserve one section for weeds; for if you do, after a time, it will no longer be a garden but a wilderness." Sow a life that will reap an abundance of sweetness without weeds of bitterness and regret.

A Nebraska monk has written about living life. He said that had he had his life to live over again he would have done things much differently.

"If I had my life to live over again, I'd try to make more mistakes next time.
I would relax, I would limber up, I would be sillier than I have been this trip.
I know of very few things I would take seriously.
I would take more trips. I would be crazier.
I would climb more mountains, swim more rivers, and watch more sunsets.
I would do more walking and looking.
I would eat more ice cream and less beans.
I would have more actual troubles, and fewer imaginary ones.
You see, I'm one of those people who live life prophylactically and sensibly hour after hour day after day. Oh, I've had my moments, and if I had to do it over again I'd have more of them.
In fact, I'd try to have nothing else, just moments, one after another, instead of living so many years ahead each day. I've been one of those people who never go anywhere without a thermometer, a hot water bottle, a raincoat, aspirin and a parachute.
If I had to do it over again I would go places, do things, and travel lighter than I have.
If I had my life to live over I would start being barefooted earlier in the spring and stay that way late in the fall.
I would play hookey more.
I would ride the merry-go-rounds.
I'd pick more daisies.

One of the reasons we do not discover the sweetness of life, as the monk did late in life, is because we worry. Worry forces us to focus on the wrong things; instead of focusing on "Whatever is true, what is honest and just, whatever is pure, lovely and excellent and what is worthy of praise...."[4]

Dr. Walter Cavert reported a survey on worry that indicated that only eight percent of the things people worried about were legitimate. The other 92 percent were either imaginary, never happened, or involved matters over which the people had no control.

Arthur Rank was a British industrialist. He had much that he could worry about. But he did not—because of what he called his "Wednesday Worry Club". Daily some worry or anxiety would arise, but instead of worrying about it, he would write it down on a piece of paper and place it in a box to be worried about on Wednesday at 4:00 p.m. At that time, he would open the box and begin to read the papers he had placed in the box. And invariably, he would find that by the time he read the piece of paper almost all the worries had been handled or were no longer important. In fact, he said, "I would find that 92 percent of my worries had failed to materialize." You might ask what he did about the other 8 percent. His reply, "I just put them back in the box to be worried about next Wednesday."

Don't let fears fill your mind; but rather, fill your mind with whatever is true, honest, pure, lovely, and excellent; and allow that to force the fear out. And then teach your children to fill their mind with the same virtue.

SOMEDAY GAME

Another reason we don't experience the sweetness of life is because we wait. We play the Someday game. We say "some day my ship will come in." "Some day I will be discovered." "Some day I will find true love." And while we wait, we waste the time we have to live our lives to the fullest.

— • —

I am reminded of my mother when she was in the last years of her life. My mother, when she was in her twenties and thirties, had collected beautiful china. Some of it was handed down to her from her mother and grandmother. All of which she kept in the china cabinet to be admired and appreciated but *never* to be used unless special company came. Most of the china was never used and some of it was actually still in the original packaging 50 years later. Even after fifty years she still was saying it was not to be used.

I remember telling her before she went in the hospital and about five years before she died. "Mom, if the company that you wanted to use those china plates for haven't come by now, then they aren't coming."

It didn't matter. It was always someday we will use it. Some day the occasion and the company worthy of it would come.

Perhaps you have something like that in your home or life. Some day I will use those tablecloths, or china tea cups. Some day I will take the trip of a lifetime. Some day I will tell that someone I love them. Some day is today. What are you waiting for?

To my mother's dying day—in hospital having been blind, paralyzed for nearly 5 years and then going deaf, my mother was adamant that those precious tea cups and china sets would not be used until the special company came.

When she died—they came. We opened the china cabinet and the boxes and used them. She never got the pleasure of using them, just admiring them.

— • —

Our life is determined not so much by what life brings to us, as much as what attitude we bring to life; not so much by what happens to us, as much as how we look at and respond to what happens to us. Remember; life is a gift—accept it. When you do, you will discover that there are *no ordinary moments.*

2

Life Isn't Fair— Do Something About it

True peace is not merely the absence of tension. It is the presence of justice. ~ *Martin Luther King Jr.*

Every child, if they are to grow into being fully realized human beings must have a sense of security. And that begins when they feel nurtured, loved and protected. I remember singing to each of my children and many of the hundreds of others who have been held close to my heart while in my arms:

Hush, little baby, don't say a word,
Daddy's going to buy you a mockingbird.
And if that mockingbird won't sing
Daddy's going to buy you a diamond ring.
If that diamond ring turns brass,
Daddy's going to buy you a looking glass.
If that looking glass gets broke,

Daddy's going to buy you a cart and bull.
And if that cart and bull turns over,
Daddy's going to buy you a dog name Rover,
If that dog named Rover won't bark,
Daddy's going to buy you a horse and cart.
If that horse and cart falls down.
You'll still be the sweetest baby in town.

Every child needs a mommy or daddy or both. They need someone to be the one to protect and provide for them no matter what happens; and in the end assure them that no matter what happens they remain in your eyes "the sweetest baby in town."

When this is provided by the parents the child has a place of safety from which to deal with the realities of life. They can know that they have that sense of security from which to begin to grow and learn the lessons of life. However, this is not always the case. I have found that life for many is not fair at all. In fact it is truly frightening. For many it is all about surviving.

LIFE ISN'T FAIR

I have discovered that for a child living in the dark world of child abuse fear becomes a way of life and survival the method of living that life. And life is not fair. It is all about survival. It is all about making the necessary compromises needed to be able to make it through another day without being beaten or abused. It is all about making the very people who might hug you one minute, and beat you until you bleed the next, happy in order to endure another day. No one ought to live like that. There must be protection provided and justice administered to outlaw this inhuman behavior. However, the laws we have are not enforced appropriately by the judges placed in authority to adjudicate the law and administer justice.

And so the child is left to fend for itself. An abused child, as a result, has to develop a form of pseudo maturity that shows itself in behaviors aimed at keeping their parents happy and content. In *The Child Called It,* Dave Pelzer describes this reality when he said of his mother, "She smeared the diaper on my face. I tried to sit perfectly still. I knew if I moved it would only be worse. I didn't look up."[5]

This is the reality of abused children. Slowly they twist and contort themselves to make themselves become almost invisible to the abusive parent. They sit still. They don't move. They don't say a word. They do not want to create any reason to see them displeased for fear that they might strike out in a violent rage or with some sick sexual urge. They do not wish to add a single ounce of pressure to their parents' life or their tormented mind for fear of what that would cause their mother, father or guardian to do to them.

As a result they take on the role of caring for themselves. For Dave Pelzer and the hundreds of children that we have cared for just like him, it meant doing things like stealing food at school so that he would not have to deal with the rages at home when he asked for food. "At night I was so hungry, my stomach growled as if I were an angry bear. I lay awake concentrating on food. 'Maybe tomorrow I'll get dinner,' I said to myself … I started stealing food at school … before school began, while my classmates were playing outside the building. I would sneak to the wall right outside my homeroom, drop my lunch pail by another pail and kneel down so nobody could see me hunting through their lunches."[6]

The problem is that this eventually backfires. They are not adults and cannot care for themselves or their younger siblings well enough to get by. In Dave's case, he was caught and the fact he was stealing was reported home and the punishment and abuse became even more severe. His mother used the fact against him that he was hungry by making him eat a full diaper. "Mother's hands seized my neck. Again she repeated, 'EAT IT!' I held my breath. The smell was overpowering. I tried to focus on the top corner of the diaper. Seconds seemed like hours. Mother must have known my plan. She slammed my face into the diaper and rubbed it from side to side."[7]

Notice he didn't fight her, none of the children do. They comply. They become pliable and malleable. They submit to the abuse for fear of something worse happening. Dave Pelzer tried even during this disgusting abuse to do what she wanted him to do so that something worse wouldn't happen. However, even that backfired because as he said, "Somehow she must have known my plan." And the worse thing did happen. His face was slammed into the diaper.

Often when one plan backfires the abused child will think of another to meet his or her needs without raising their parent's awareness or attracting further abuse. When Dave was caught stealing food at school and it was reported to his mother he couldn't do that anymore so he began to steal from stores. However, when he brought the food home he again got caught. He said, "The manager called Mother. At the house, I was thrashed relentlessly. Mother knew why I stole food and so did Dad, but she still refused to feed me. The more I craved food, the more I tried to come up with a better plan to steal it."[8]

The plotting and planning is part of the survival and pseudo maturing process that each abused child undertakes when trying to survive without being abused. This inhumanity to the most fragile human beings amongst us is not fair and demands a response.

LIFE ISN'T FAIR—DO SOMETHING ABOUT IT!

Children have a very acute sense of what is fair and unfair. I have heard my children, on more then one occasion, say when faced with experiencing some inequality, "Daddy, that is not fair!" I would agree, and then say "Darling, life isn't always fair. Get use to it or do something about it."

That may be harsh, but it's true. For all the talk today about equality—life isn't equal. We may want it to be, but that doesn't make it that way. Some children are born into wealth, while others know only poverty. Other children are born in countries where freedom from slavery is the reality, while others find themselves enslaved in countries in other parts of the world. Still others are born into war-torn countries while we in Canada, and the United States, are born and raised free from the daily terror of war and abject poverty. Daily many children are abused or neglected while still others are raised in an environment of love and nurturing. Life isn't fair, nor is it equal. We don't have to like it—I don't—but we have to deal with it.

My wife Liane and I have chosen to do something about it by opening our home and hearts to children who have not been given the nurturing and love that we have. The world is filled with injustice, but we can strive to make an unjust world a little more just.

We have chosen to do that by intentionally opening our home to abused children and doing so with our children's involvement. We wanted them to learn to be more humane. We want them to learn to be a blessing in this broken world. I have always believed that anyone can make a difference. Anyone can change the world. It really doesn't matter how young or old, or big or small you are.

I remember reading the story of the *Lion and the Mouse* by

Aesop to my children when they were little to teach them this important lesson.

"One day a great lion lay asleep in the sunshine. A little mouse ran across his paw and wakened him. The great lion was about to eat him up when the little mouse cried, 'Oh, please, let me go, Sir. Some day I may help you.'

"The lion laughed at the thought that the little mouse could be of any use to him. But he was a good-natured lion, and set the mouse free.

"Not long after, the lion was caught in a net. He tugged and pulled with all his might, but the ropes were too strong. Then he roared loudly. The little mouse heard him and ran to the spot. 'Be still, dear lion, and I will set you free. I will gnaw the ropes.'

"With his sharp little teeth, the mouse cut the ropes, and the lion came out of the net.

"'You laughed at me once,' said the mouse. 'You thought I was too little to do you a good turn. But see, you owe your life to a poor little mouse.'"

Like the little mouse, little children too can do a "good turn"."

My children are truly amazing because they have been willing to freely and lovingly do a good turn. They put up with a great deal due to our decision to care for the hundreds of children in need. Yet, they remain surprisingly normal. And yes, they complain like all other children about how things are not fair. However, now they also do something to even things up.

I found this list of lessons about real life that I gave to my children after I had finally had enough of their complaining about life not being fair for them. It is attributed to Bill Gates:

Rule 1: Life is not fair—get used to it!

Rule 2: The world won't care about your self-esteem. The world will expect you to accomplish something BEFORE you feel good about yourself.

Rule 3: You will NOT make $60,000 a year right out of high school. You won't be a vice-president with a car phone until you earn both.

Rule 4: If you think your teacher is tough, wait till you get a boss.

Rule 5: Flipping burgers is not beneath your dignity. Your grandparents had a different world for burger flipping—they called it opportunity.

Rule 6: If you mess up, it's not your parents' fault, so don't whine about your mistakes, learn from them.

Rule 7: Before you were born, your parents weren't as boring as they are now. They got that way from paying your bills, cleaning your clothes and listening to you talk about how cool you thought you were. So before you save the rain forest from the parasites of your parent's generation, try delousing the closet in your own room.

Rule 8: Your school may have done away with winners and losers, but life HAS NOT. In some schools they have abolished failing grades and they'll give you as many times as you need to get the right answer. This doesn't bear the lightest resemblance to anything in real life.

Rule 9: Life does not divide into semesters. You don't get summers off and very few employers are interested in helping you to find yourself. Do that on your own time.

Rule 10: Television is not real life. In real life people actually have to leave the coffee shop and go to jobs.

Rule 11: Be nice to nerds. Chances are you'll end up working for one.

These rules are true to life. The world doesn't care about your self-esteem or your complaints that life isn't fair. That is just the way it is. However, it is our responsibility as we teach our children to become more human and humane to try their best to right the inequalities wherever possible. This is the lesson I learned from the children we have cared for. It isn't fair that children are forced to face the torment of abuse and mistreatment. It isn't fair that children are not protected by the laws we have in place for that purpose. It isn't fair that we don't have better laws. Yet, the one thing we must never do is give up. We must continue striving for change.

Greek philosopher Diogenes commented that there are three things which are most difficult to do. The first is to keep a secret. The second is to find a useful way to spend one's leisure, and the third is to accept an injustice.

I agree except with respect to leisure. With eight children and all the others we have cared for I don't think I have had any leisure time to worry about spending usefully.

Injustice is never to be accepted. But to understand what injustice is one has to know what justice truly means. The most effective and simple definition of justice is given by some of the great philosophical minds throughout history. Philosophers like Homer, Plato, Aristotle, St. Augustine, St. Thomas Aquinas, Cicero, and the **Corpus Juris Civilis** of Roman law (Instit. I,I) all use the same definition when speaking of justice. Homer cites it in the **Odyssey** (14,84), Plato in the Republic, Aristotle in the Rhetoric (1,9), Cicero in De finibus (5,23), St. Augustine in **City of God** (19,21), and St. Thomas Aquinas in his **Commentaries on Aristotle's Ethics** (5,1; no. 893). The Latin expression of this definition is "**suum cuique**" or "to everyone their due." An "injustice" means someone has not been given their due or what is their right.

I thought again of what is a child's human right when I read about an eight-year-old boy who committed suicide three days after he was taken out of foster care and reunited with his birth father and four siblings. "Manitoba's chief Medical Examiner said yesterday he is seeking answers into the March 28, 2005 death of Henry Willard Okemow found hanging in a closet in a home on God's Lake Narrows...He apparently told his family he was going to hang himself."[9] The Awasis Agency, a provincial child welfare organization formed in 1983 that serves 12 remote communities in northern Manitoba "...came under criticism last year by a provincial inquest judge for its handling of a 15 year old girl who committed suicide days after she was sent back to her family, that includes a stepfather just released from jail for sexually abusing her. Shamattawa resident Susan Redhead ended her life by hanging herself in February, 2000. Judge Mary Curtis found child-welfare officials failed the teen, and Awasis officials admitted at the inquest their philosophy of trying to reunite families was not appropriate in the case."[10] The missing element in this case is justice and in so many others as well. It is easy to blame the child welfare officials, but where was the judge? The judge is the gatekeeper for child protection, all too often sends children back to the abusive home with little consideration at all of the child's welfare. As I stated in my book, *How I Became Father To 1000 Children and the Lessons Learned* there was a baby by the name of Sara Coa who lived for 39 days. She had 10 fractured ribs. Some of the broken ribs were old injuries and were not caused by the final brutal and violent abuse that in the end killed her. Yet, the Judge simply slapped the mother who killed her, on the wrist, and sent her home. The Judge seemed to almost apologize to the women who killed her child for having made her stay in jail for 22 days while she awaited trial. He viewed himself and the crown attorney and the defense lawyer as having a "more reasonable and enlightened assessment of the public interest…" by not even having her kept under house arrest. Even Martha Stewart served 5 months in jail and 5 months under house arrest. And what was Martha Stewart's crime—murder? No. She lied under oath. There is something wrong in the world when a person who lies under oath gets a 10 month jail sentence and someone who murders a child gets no time in jail. And this is called justice! I tell you this not to depress you but to remind you that a world without true justice is a world out of control.

Justice means having one's rights respected by others. It means not being oppressed or taken advantage of. When justice is administered appropriately it can be seen as creating fairness, equality and harmony. When relationships are based on these three things then we have a better community. This takes work and often is accompanied by both resistance and interference. And sometimes we are left with an overwhelming sense of futility.

I have at times wondered if anything can be done to bring about a more humane and just world. I find hope as I see my children grow—and the many children who we have seen move through our home for adoption—grow into wonderful loving humane human beings. I also have been encourage by a poem by Kent Keith *Anyway*.

Kent Keith wrote *Anyway* that speaks of the importance of accepting the reality of life as it is but doing what needs to be done anyway.

People are unreasonable, illogical and self-centered
—love them anyway.
If you do good, people may accuse you of selfish motives
—do good anyway.
If you are successful, you may win false friends and true enemies—succeed anyway.
The good you do today may be forgotten tomorrow
—do good anyway.
Honesty and frankness make you vulnerable
—be honest and frank anyway.
What you spend years building may be destroyed over night
—build anyway.
People who really want help may attack you if you help them
—help them anyway.
Give the world the best you have and you may get kicked in the teeth—give the world the best anyway.

People can be unfriendly, frustrating and foolish—accept them anyway. This is what I learned from my children as they easily welcomed all the others into their home and heart.

Most of us have had, at one time or another, someone betray us. We learned then that life can be brutal. Too often we have to face an unfriendly environment, unpleasant circumstances, unreasonable people or an uncertain future. What do we do then?

DO GOOD ANYWAY

In the face of an unfriendly environment—do good anyway. It has always been my desire that my children might learn the importance of blessing other people. The world can be an unfriendly place. However, we can experience the beauty and the majesty of life when we seek to be a blessing.

Do you remember Kathleen Ferrier? She was much loved, a superb contralto, who died of cancer while still a young woman. She was once rehearsing Gustov Mahler's *"Das lied von der Erde"* with Bruno Walter when the beauty and pathos of the words and music overwhelmed her. She couldn't go on and the conductor had to call a break in the rehearsal. Miss Ferrier apologized to Bruno Walter, but he replied "Kathleen, you have nothing for which to apologize we should have all been weeping."

She understood as Blake did that,

Joy and Woe are woven fine
A clothing of soul divine
Underneath each grief and pine
Runs a joy of silken twine
And when this we rightly know
Safely through the world we go

There is much in this world that can move us to tears. Much that ought to move us to make a difference and be a blessing.

A two year old little girl fell out of a seventh story building and lived. She and her brothers and sister were left to fend for themselves most of the time. There was no food or clothing in the house. They were eating feces on the ground in their hunger. It was her falling out of the seven-story window that finally brought the desperate plight of her and her brothers and sister to light.

When Lilly came to us from the hospital she was in what could only be described as a body cast. She was delayed mentally due to lack of stimulation and nurturing. I watched as my oldest daughter Alyssa, who was 17 at the time, asked to go to "Sick Kids" hospital with my wife, while I stayed with the babies. She wanted to be there to bring her home. With pride I gaze at how tenderly she carried Lilly into her new home and tended to her every need over the next day. She placed her in a wheelchair and took her outside to sit in the sun and walk her around the block.

Alyssa knows all too well, as we do, that the good we do today for Lilly, may in a few months—if she is sent home to the same situation—be undone. But she chooses to do good anyway. That is what it means to learn to be human and humane.

REMAIN POSITIVE ANYWAY

In the face of unpleasant circumstances always remain positive. I remember hearing about a little boy who was overhead talking to himself as he strode through the backyard, baseball cap in place and toting ball and bat, "I'm the greatest baseball player in the world." Then he tossed the ball in the air, swung and missed. Undaunted, he picked up the ball, threw it into the air and said, to himself, "I'm the greatest player ever!" he swung at the ball, and again he missed. He paused a moment to examine the bat and the ball carefully. Then one more time he threw the ball in the air and said, "I'm the greatest baseball player in the world." He swung and missed. "Wow," he said, "What a pitcher!"

He had the right attitude. Our outlook determines our altitude and only we can choose our attitude.

Victor Frankel a survivor of a Nazi death camp and psychologist said, "The last of the human freedoms is to choose one's attitude in any given set of circumstances."

James Allen says, "You are today where your thoughts have brought you; you will be tomorrow where your thoughts take you."

Sacred Parenting is about helping and encouraging our

children to choose how they respond to any situation. It is about instilling in them the understanding that they can choose their attitude. It is about equipping them to live above circumstances. We have all heard it said, "I'm fine considering the circumstances I'm in." A sacred parent helps the child to respond to the circumstance and rise above them, and never to accept to live under them.

For four decades East Berlin was controlled by the Communists. West Berlin was free. One day a few people who lived in East Berlin took a truckload of garbage and dumped it on the West Berlin side. The people of West Berlin could have retaliated by doing the same thing. But instead they took a truckload of canned goods, bread, and milk and neatly stacked it on the East Berlin side. On top of this stack of food they placed the sign: "Each gives what he has."

BE ACCEPTING ANYWAY

In the face of unreasonable people—be accepting of them anyway. It is not always easy for us to be accepting of parents who have violently abused and starved their children. It is difficult for us to be accepting of those who have intentionally broken their children's legs and arms or burned them with cigarettes.

What has helped us to be more accepting is by understanding what they went through in their lives. Though we are there to protect the children, we do come in contact with their parents. It is easy to be judgmental. It is easy to want to reject them. To be sure they chose to abuse. To be sure they could have chosen to get help. And for not doing so they have lost the right to have their child and perhaps lose the right to ever see them again if they continue in that self-destructive path and refuse the help that is being offered. However, if we act towards them as inhumanely as they did to their children then we are no better. On some level we must accept them anyway. We must offer them, what they were perhaps never offered.

The world can be cruel and callous. People need a place of comfort. Everyone needs a soft place to land.

Pepper Rogers was said to be having an awful year coaching his team. Everywhere he went people were condemning him for the job he was doing. Everyone—family, friends and neighbors—were disgusted with the way the team was playing and how he was coaching. Finally, after a particularly perplexing day where nothing went right, he came home and said to his wife in hopes of some comfort and acceptance, "Darling, I've only got one friend in the world and I need two." So she went out and bought him a dog. Now that's cruel and cold. But at least his dogs will love and accept him. Some people can't even have that.

LOVE ANYWAY

In the face of uncertain future you can love anyway. When we stop focusing on the problems and start focusing on the underlying purpose, everything starts to become easier.

We live in a world where people are lost and alone; where people are looking for love in all the wrong places.

People search for love as if it were a city lost beneath the desert dunes. Each child rediscovers it, each couple redefines it, each parent reinvents it. The word can mean nothing, or it can mean everything. We say it in relation to things we eat and wear, and to those we eat with. We say, "I love Baskin and Robin's ice cream." "I love that sweater." "I'd love to go skiing." Or "Daddy loves you." It can be such a sloppy word. Yet, it can be so wonderful.

"How much do you love me?" a child asks. And we say as we fling open our arms and stretch out our fingers to try to grasp the world and bring it in, "I love you this much!" When Elizabeth Barrett Browning wrote her famous sonnet, "How Do I Love Thee?" she didn't "count the ways" because she had a mind for math, but because as an English poet she was trying to convey and search for ways to tell of her fondness for her beloved husband.

Love is powerful. We all seek to have it. We all need it. Love is perhaps the basic human need. Someone once said that "Life minus love is zero." The great psychiatrist, Karl Menninger, declared that "Love cures people—both the ones who give it and the ones who receive it." And we are probably all familiar with the quote by the Roman statesman and philosopher, Lucius Annaeus Seneca, who lived at the time of Christ. He said, "Better to have loved and lost than never to have loved at all." And throughout history people have written about, sung about, and thought about love more than perhaps any other single human need. It has been sung, "What the world needs now is love."

A professor once asked, "What is love?" A student replied, "Love is dancing cheek to cheek amidst stardust." Another said, "Life is one thing after another. Love is two things after each other." A third quipped, "Love is a feeling you feel, when you feel you're going to feel a feeling you never felt before."

However, one is left with the thought that love is only a feeling. And that is when we get into trouble because when the diapers have to be changed—and as a father I know what I'm talking about and then the garbage has to be taken out and the dishes have to be done; the feeling you felt, when you felt you were going to feel a feeling you never felt before vanishes. And you wonder if love is only a feeling. It is not. It is a choice we make and a commitment we take to heart. That is a lesson that every child needs to learn—and to live.

CELEBRATE ANYWAY

In the face of confusing circumstances—celebrate anyway. Too often when we are faced with injustice we allow it to confuse us, frustrate us and stop us from celebrating life. We simply endure life as a result. We don't enjoy it. We don't stop to take pleasure in the simple things of life. Celebrate what you can do. Celebrate what you have done. Simply celebrate.

LEARN ANYWAY

In the face of unhappy times—be open to learning anyway. We all know that one of the main problems about traveling by car is that no matter what, you always get into an area where there is construction. I read a sign a rather wise construction worker placed on the grader he was driving. "The road to happiness is almost always under construction."

The same applies not only to roads but to our lives and the lives that we lead. It is one that had detours and difficulties, pot holes and problems and is not always smooth.

Who hasn't heard, "no pain, no gain". How true. Each week I work out in a gym. And every time I go, I see people in pain—and I'm one of them. And every day, I try to convince myself that this is good pain.

I've been told, "But John there are different kinds of pain, and this is good pain."

I looked at him and said, "What psych ward were you just let out of. Good pain?" He was later proven right.

We all know a physical workout produces pain because muscles are being stretched to their limit. This is a gift to the body, for it produces greater strength and health when the muscle recovers. It is the same for the spiritual as the physical. God allows the pain to come into our life, to produce a greater spiritual gain for us.

C.S. Lewis commented, "God whispers to us in our pleasure and shouts at us in our pain. Pain is the megaphone to rouse a dulled world." Often we notice God, only after something difficult happens. When the pain comes, it is often only then that we pursue God.

St. Teresa of Avila said it simply, "Everything is grace." If this is true; then the good gifts are grace, because they are a part of everything—but then suffering is grace too, because it is something. Is this hard to accept? For most of us everything in us wants to refuse this fact. We don't want to accept that God could be allowing some suffering in our lives—not that suffering comes from God, but He allows it to occur to work out His purpose—His will in us. So everything remains grace only in the hands of God. It is grace only as it calls us to God.

A saying from the bible tells us, "All things work together for good." Notice that St. Paul did not say, that all things are good—far from it. There are many things that are not good in life. But if we allow God into them, He will make good from what is bad.

Although Henri Mattise was nearly 28 years younger than Auguste Renoir, the two great artists were dear friends and frequent companions. When Renoir was confined to his home during the last decade of his life Mattise visited him daily. Renoir, almost paralyzed by arthritis, continued to paint in spite of his infirmities. One day as Matisse watched the elder painter working in his studio, fighting torturous pain with each brush stroke, he blurted out: "Auguste, why do you continue to paint when you are in such agony?"

Renoir answered simply; "The pain passes, but the beauty remains."

When we truly grasp this, it is then that we understand that there are *no ordinary moments.*

3

Life Is Hard—Deal With It

Fear not that your life will come to an end but that it will never have had a beginning. ~ *John Henry Newman*

Courage is not just an acquired virtue but a required one. Courage is, of course, admired by everyone; just as cowardice is equally despised. Courage is the ability to overcome fear and move forward. It is not the absence of fear but the willingness to master it and move through it The ancient philosophers and thinkers believed that courage was one of the foundational virtues. Thomas Aquinas spoke of courage as *fortitude* which was a moral strength, and "a condition of every virtue."[11] Aristotle said, "It is requisite for every virtue to act firmly and immovably," however Cicero points out it remains a "deliberate facing of dangers and bears toils."[12] This means that courage at its root denotes moral strength against a wrong done as well as being able to face up to and bear the dangers and troubles that that may bring. I think of the courage it required for a little five year old boy to escape the terror of his home with his baby brother in his arms. He had finally come to the point in his short life that he believed he had to act for the welfare of himself and his little brother. While his abusive parents were asleep in a drunken stupor he escaped into the shadows of night carrying his baby brother in his arms. They were found by strangers who called the police, who in turn called Children's Aid, who then called us.

His eyes darted like a caged animal looking for a way out when he arrived in our home. He didn't know that our home would be any different than the place from which he had just escaped. He refused to realize that he was now out of the torment. All he felt was fear that he remained in danger. He kept looking warily for a way out, eyes darting back and forth. After feeding, bathing and putting him and his brother into clean new pajamas we placed them in bed to sleep. It didn't take long for him to act. We heard the shattering glass as Liane and I made our way downstairs. We ran into the room to find him lunging out of a broken window onto the roof. I grabbed him by his leg before he fell off the roof and got hurt on the ground below. We checked to see if there were any cuts from the glass. Fortunately he was unhurt. We called a friend who installs windows who brought a temporary one for the night, and came the next day and installed a new one.

That night we stayed close to the boy until he fell asleep. The next day, he had calmed down and seemed to begin to be less tormented as he played with the other children.

Courage is not the absence of fear. It is the recognition that one needs to act in spite of the fear. This little child believed he needed to act for his and his brother's safety. And the fear of the dark and the unknown was less frightening than the fear of the known.

"Courage," said Winston Churchill, "is rightly esteemed the first of human qualities ... because it is the quality which guarantees all others." It is the quality that determines whether you push forward or fall back.

Life expands in direct proportion to your courage. Fear limits leaders. The Roman historian Tacitus wrote, "The desire for safety stands against every great and noble enterprise." Courage, however, opens doors. Courage not only gives a better beginning, but a brighter future, and a blessed end. Obstacles became stepping stones when courage is operating; closed doors hide open windows; rejections give opportunity for practice, and precision. The storm always serves as an opportunity to save lives when courage is present.

Marya Sklodowska loved school and learning. It was what caused her to always want to get to the heart of matter. As a child growing up in Poland, when her parents lost their teaching jobs and took in boarders to survive, and despite the fact that she would spend endless hours helping with the chores; she still finished first in her high school class. Amazingly her exams were not even taken in her native tongue. They were in Russian.

She became a tutor as well as a governess since the door to higher education was closed to her. During this time she squirreled away enough money to send her older sister through medical school in Paris. Then she also moved to France to study at the Sorbonne. After three years of study she earned a Master's degree in mathematics and finished first in her class in physics. She focused her attention on research that included experiments for the French industrial society. However, she had a secret passion for the study of uranium and its rays.

Marya, while looking for a better laboratory to do her research and studies, met the man who would later become her husband and research partner, Pierre. You've probably heard of Marya Sklodoska, but it's likely that you learned the name she preferred after she married Pierre Curie in 1895, and became known as Madame Marie Curie.

Madame Curie continued her research and went on to do groundbreaking work in the field of radioactivity (a term she coined). She was the catalyst that opened the door to the study of nuclear physics and modern medical radiology.

"Life is not easy for any of us," she once said, "but what of that? We must have perseverance and above all courage and confidence in ourselves. We must believe that we are gifted for something and that this thing must be attained." Her research brought her great recognition: fifteen gold medals, nineteen degrees, and two Nobel prizes (one in physics and one in chemistry.) During WWI she noted what was happening on the battle fields and recognized that the technology she had discovered could save lives. She and her daughter Irene (who would later also win the Nobel prize) developed the X-ray equipment and later led a movement to equip ambulances with them. Curie trained 150 technicians to use it, and founded the Radium Institute at the University of Paris.

She said, "Nothing in life is to be feared. It is only to be understood."

Nothing stopped her. She knew that with courage, obstacles become stepping stones; closed doors shield us from open windows, rejections only give opportunity for practice, and precision.

In the city of Jerusalem just as "Desert Shield" became "Desert Storm", Zubin Mehta was conducting the Israel Philharmonic Orchestra with Isaac Stern as soloist, when the sirens sounded, warning that a Scud missile was on its way. If it was not intercepted it would certainly explode and might release poison gas or germs. The members of the audience put on their gas masks, and the orchestra left the stage.

Then, says the *New York Times,* with "awesome courage" Isaac Stern returned and played his violin, and what he played was Bach's Saraband for Solo Violin affirming the triumph of civilization and order over chaos and death.

LIFE IS HARD—DEAL WITH IT

Life is hard! And it can hurt! That is why it takes courage to live and learn to be truly human. Karl Barth, a Swiss theologian has commented, "Courage is fear that has said its prayers."

It is easy to give up and turn to something like alcohol, drugs, food or something else to self-medicate as a way to avoid dealing with the way things are; but it takes courage to be self-motivated to move forward in spite of the fear. Everyone prefers to avoid the pain and the crises in life. Yet, the irony for most of us is that we learn the most valuable things during the most trying times. You may have heard or said yourself, "I wouldn't go through that again, if you paid me a million dollars. But I would never trade what I learned for anything."

LOOK FOR THE LESSON

As parents we need to empower our children to begin to deal with the hard times that they will eventually have to face by equipping them to look for the lesson. Recall that St. Teresa says simply, "Everything is grace." If this is true; then the good gifts are grace, because they are part of everything—but then suffering is grace, because it is something. I know that this is very hard to accept. It was hard for me, too. Everything in us wants to refuse this fact. We don't want to accept the fact that God could be allowing some to suffer—not that suffering comes from God, but that suffering is in the world and He allows it to occur—to work out His purpose in us.

It is often when we have a brush with death that we become more acutely aware of life. It is when we suffer that we often begin to see more clearly. For it is then that the unimportant things slip away and we become aware of what really is important.

The great spiritual leaders never ask, "Why do bad things happen to good people?" Why? They know that bad things affect God's people; because, God uses the bad things to produce better people.

It is not that pain is good, but that God is good and His grace is sufficient for us. Everything is then valuable not vanity. Everything is meaningful not meaningless. Of course, we can not possibly know the meaning of every event, but we can know that every event has meaning and therefore is meaningful.

"Everything happens for a reason." Another way of saying "everything is Grace."

No one gets through this life without bruises. That is why as parents, who understand their sacred trust, we seek to instill courage in our children. This comes only through the knowledge that though life is hard and it hurts, it is no excuse to give up, but becomes the reason to get up and deal with it, not to run from it.

Sacred Parenting throughout the whole difficult time assures the children they are not alone in their struggle. The children, with parents who understand their sacred responsibility, assure their children that they not only have their parents who seek to love and protect them, but they also have God who is watching over them and will bring some later good out of it. This prayer speaks to us about this.

"I asked God for strength, that I might achieve,
I was made weak that I might learn humbly to obey.
I asked for health, that I might do greater things.
I was given infirmity, that I might do better things.
I asked for riches, that I might be happy,
I was given poverty, that I might be wise.
I asked for power, that I might have the praise of men,
I was given weakness, that I might feel the need for God.
I asked for all things, that I might enjoy life.
I was given life, that I might enjoy all things.
I got nothing I asked for—but everything that I had hoped for
Almost despite myself, my unspoken prayers were answered.
I am among all men most richly blessed."

LOOK FOR WAYS TO LIFT

St. Thomas More tells us, "The times are never so bad that a good man cannot live in them." We know we live in difficult times. This message shouts at us from the TV and screams from newspaper headlines. As parents and grandparents, teachers and leaders it is frightening to think of what is out there for our children. We fear for their safety, their survival, and their very souls. With bullying on the rise, and children killing children, it can be terrifying for parents to think about sending their child out into the world. Often we wonder if they will make it through this life whole, and healthy. It is not like when we were in school. The teen years are not easy for any child however, the challenges that the children have to face today are far more difficult than I ever remember having to deal with. The brutality of the times seems to have reached right into our children at schools and homes.

A survey of school principals in the late 1940s asked this: "What are the main problems among your students? The reply?

1. Not doing homework
2. Chewing gum
3. Running in the halls
4. Making noise
5. Cutting in line
6. Dress code infractions
7. Littering

In 1990 a survey asked the same question. The answer?

1. Drugs
2. Alcohol abuse
3 Rape
4. Pregnancy
5. Suicide
6 Robbery
7. Assault[13]

Our concerns for our children are not illusionary. They are real. It, therefore, demands a response.

The stark and shocking reality of this came home to me again when I was called to visit and care for the family whose son and two friends had created a "hit list" of students at school whom they were going to kill, but first he would wipe out his whole family.

The call came after he brutally assaulted and nearly killed his stepfather and did kill his brother. Unbeknownst to him an old girl friend had reported him to the police being concerned that he might actually go through with the threats he had told her about. The sad truth was she was too late. It was only through the stepfather's shear force of will to live that he thwarted the plans of the killers and saved his life and the lives of the others. His only regret is that he did not arrive home soon enough to stop the senseless murder of his younger stepson.

After officiating at his brother's funeral, I visited the boy in jail. It is my impression that his desire was to wipe out his past before continuing on his rampage to kill the bullies and his tormentors at school before ending his future. The only blessing is that he was unable to get a gun to do the killing due to the strong gun laws in Canada. If he had access to a gun I believe it would have been another Columbine massacre. Instead, he and his buddies used bats, knives and machetes to end the bright future of his wonderful and loving12 year-old brother.

The concerns are real; the responsibility real. It is the sacred responsibility of the parent to equip their child to face the future without fear, to effectively deal with the issues they must as they pass through life. At the same time it is the responsibility of the parent to raise children who honor the lives of others and not bully and brutalize them until those "geeks, nerds, outcasts" give up all hope and become what they themselves have despised. There is a reason that when the gun was first created in the old west that it was called the "Equalizer" because it leveled the playing field. No longer could a big bully get away with picking on a small guy. A small man or woman with a gun was as strong or stronger than a big guy with muscles and a mouth.

This must change. We must begin to encourage positive behavior and support, honor, and reward good deeds. One way to do this is through simple encouragement. The word encouragement contains "courage" at its centre—it literally means to give courage. We give courage when we encourage. There are many reasons in life that children get discouraged. The worst is when they feel that they have no one that they can turn to when they are having trouble or when they are in trouble. The worst possible situation is when a child feels they are totally alone. Does yours? Ask them, you may be surprised at the answer.

This is what happened for Thomas Monaghan, the founder of Domino's Pizza. His success was due to one very special person in his life. After his father died and his mother faced financial problems, he and his brother Jim were placed in St. Joseph's Orphanage in Jackson, Michigan. He lived there for six years. While there his big dreams were continually encouraged by Sister Mary Berarda. She knew that encouragement makes all the difference. "Have faith in God, and have faith in yourself. Then go out and do it. You can be anything you want to be." She came to every baseball game, was a supporter whenever she could be. She read him books and stories about famous people, like Henry Ford, Stanley Marcus of Neiman Marcus and Ray Kroc, the founder of McDonald's, she showed him that it doesn't matter how little one has to start with as long as they start.

Monaghan spent four years in the Marine Corps and after going back into civilian life opened a newsstand. He was in the midst of expanding it when his brother called and said he had a chance to buy a Pizza parlor called Dominicks in Ypsilanti, Michigan and wanted Monaghan to help him run it.

Under his management, the parlor soon went from a five-hundred dollar a month loss to a profit. They soon expanded to a second location and the rest of the story of the Domino's Pizza outlets you know.[14]

Encouragement was the key to overcoming. We need to encourage children to expand and strive to achieve their heart's desires. However, there are things that stand in the way. It is vitally important that they not only have encouragement but an example of how to do what they want to do. Children need our encouragement but they also need our example. Children need mentors, leaders, teachers and parents to make a stand for what is right and against what is wrong. Whenever an adult achieves this—whenever they have understood their sacred trust to do so—the children have been the beneficiaries.

Rosa Parks, Martin Luther King Jr., Mother Teresa, Nelson Mandela, and countless other people have in the past made a stand for what was right. Each and every one looked for a way to lighten the burdens of others and free them from bondage whether that was the bondage of poverty, segregation, racism, or Aparthied. Each had someone in their prior life who understood their sacred responsibility of instilling this virtue and value of courage and justice within them. As a result the world they lived within was changed for the better.

Children need our encouragement, and they need our example to help them. It is foolish to say, "Do what I say, not what I do." That never works. The fact that children of parents who smoke are 80% more likely to smoke than children of none smokers proves that "Do what I say and not what I do," doesn't work. We must first show what to do. We must have the courage to stand up for the underdog and to accomplish what is right.

4

Life Is Chaotic—Balance It

Some people think that the little things don't matter. But they do. Sometimes it is the little things that bring order to disorder, and balance to chaos. Let me prove that with this little saying.

For want of a nail a shoe was lost
For want of a shoe a horse was lost
For want of a horse a rider was lost
For want of rider a message was lost
For want of a message a battle was lost
For want of a battle a kingdom was lost
And all for want of a horseshoe nail.

Little things can make a big difference. A little thing like self-discipline helps people not to lie, cheat or steal. It helps people live lives with honor and order. Self-discipline brings order to chaos. It brings balance to imbalance. When one is ruled by their passions or obsessions eventual despair and self-destruction is the result. That is why a parent who wants the best for their child will seek to instill self-discipline in their child.

Self-discipline is not something we like to hear about in the western world. In this overweight, and over-indulged society, self-discipline reminds us of the ultimate four-letter word—diet.

I hate this word as much as you do. I have lost so much weight over the years that it would equal the weight of three or four people. No matter how much I loose, some of it always finds its way back to me. Twenty years ago I weighed 300 lbs. I decided I had had enough and wanted to loose weight. I chose to learn about what was healthy for me and chose the healthier way. As a result I lost over 100 pounds.

When we instill in our children the wisdom of self-discipline we have blessed them with the beginning of a bright future. Self-discipline is a gift we give to our children that helps them manage their lives in a manner that will bear fruit long into the future. It helps them foresee the consequence of every action they take. It helps them understand their limits and controls their appetites and behaviors. The wisdom of self-discipline directs them to reach for what is right and say no to what is wrong. It gives them charge over their lives instead of allowing others or things to control them through fear, worry or need for approval, guilt or regret. It allows them to keep their act together rather then being told to "get with it".

One of the challenges of being a parent of other people's children is helping a child who has lived in chaos cope with being in a place of calm. It begins by lovingly but clearly defining what behavior is acceptable and what is not.

When a child lives in violence, violence becomes their mode of being. We allow no violence in our home. That is a firm rule.

Should one of the children strike out at another while playing, they are separated and settled down and reminded of the "no hitting" rule. For a time they sit without playing with toys or the other children. When reintroduced to playing they are again reminded of the rule. This natural and logical consequence of separation from others and instruction of the rules eventually takes hold and they begin to control their own actions, anger and behavior themselves because they do not want to be removed from having fun or playing with the other children.

DEFINITION OF SELF-CONTROL

Self-control is the internal ability to control one's own actions. The Greek from which we get our word self-control means "holding himself in." This may happen through an awareness of outside rules and required behaviors that have been internalized to form mental and emotional blocks to inappropriate behaviors and which result in making responsible decisions.

This can happen through socialization and education. Once self-control becomes a habit the behavior becomes less a response to rules and regulations and more a character trait that continues to be developed and strengthened.

THE IMPORTANCE OF SELF-CONTROL

Though I am the first one to laugh and enjoy the spontaneity and sheer joy of having children respond transparently to a given situation; however, it may really be the reality of a parent who has not taken seriously the need for their child to understand what is or isn't appropriate. It may be humorous for a three year-old to make a funny comment about a family member's physical appearance; it becomes rude and cruel for a nine year old to say the same thing. Intent is the key to understand the difference.

When a three year old makes such a comment, it becomes a teaching moment to instruct the child about what is appropriate and how such things can hurt the feelings of other people.

Children need to learn self-control regarding their words and behaviors without which behavior problems will become evident and hard to manage later. This helps to socialize the child to what is appropriate behavior.

THE DANGER OF EXCESSIVE SELF-CONTROL

There is always the danger of being excessive. There are moments when everyone ought to be given permission to be foolish. Sometimes we take ourselves too seriously and need the space just to play.

If a person is too rigid the result will be that they will eventually be unable to experience spontaneous joy. At the same time there is the risk that they will break free from what they think is the bondage of self-control and became self-destructive.

PRINCIPLE OF SELF-CONTROL

Self-control is about having a proper balance in life. When we lose control or lose our balance, many things can go wrong. We know about road rage and now there is air rage where people are put in prison for violence while on an airplane.

Eric Zorn of the Chicago Tribune wrote of a tragic accident

that occurred because of a lack of self control. A man and woman were driving a van in the far left lane of Chicago's Northwest Toll way. In the back were their two children. A white Cadillac pulled up behind closely tailgating them. The man driving the van slowed down. The Cadillac driver pulled into the right lane, passed the van, and then swerved suddenly back in front of the van. The van had to swerve to avoid a collision. The white Cadillac sped away. That could have been the end of it. But the van driver gave chase. He eventually pulled alongside the white Cadillac and began yelling and screaming. According to a witness, the two men gestured angrily at each other. The driver of the Cadillac pulled a gun and fired. The bullet entered the side of the van and hit his little girl in the head. The girl lived, but she was blind and partially deaf, and has severe disabilities as a result. The man who fired the bullet is in jail. How would you like to be the parents of the girl who must live with the terrible regret?

Road rage and of its tragic results—lives were shattered, because of the loss of self-control. The principle of self-control reminds us that it is the meek not the miserable that are blessed.

FROM BAD TO WORSE

Have you noticed that sometimes things just go from bad to worse? It is almost as if you are caught in rapids and are unable to use your paddle to steer to safety.

A few years ago a Toronto lawyer was convicted of conspiring to possess counterfeit United States Money. It all started when he began to gamble to pay off his mounting debts. Soon it became compulsive and he would sit with two radios and two television sets going at the same time to keep track of the sporting events on which he had wagered. Then he found himself in the hands of loan sharks who made threats on his life as well as on the lives of his wife and children. His last desperate attempt to pay them off was to turn to counterfeit money—only to be caught, to be fined, jailed and lose his license to practice law. Here was a man trapped in a flow, a flow of troubles that began so simply and was compounded by one awful decision after another which ruined another family who were eventually added to the waste bin of life. With each dreadful decision his troubles deepened and his fall into disgrace became complete.

This was the result of the lack of self-control. And it began for this lawyer when he made one small bet. It was just a little thing, but in his compulsion to get even, it lead to a final destructive difference.

SELF-CONTROL IS ABOUT HONORING THE RIGHT THING

In *Imaginary Homelands,* the author Salman Rushdie writes of one of his family traditions:

"In our house, whenever anyone dropped a book, it was required to be not only picked up but also kissed, by way of apology for the act of clumsy disrespect. I was as careless and butterfingered as any child, and accordingly I kissed a large number of books. Devout households in India still contain persons in the habit of kissing holy books. But we kissed everything. We kissed dictionaries, and atlases. We kissed novels and Superman comics. If I'd ever dropped the telephone directory, I'd probably have kissed that too."

Is it any surprise that Salman Rushdie grew up to become an author? What we honor defines us.

Too many people honor the wrong thing. Today the seven deadly sins have become the seven delightful virtues. Our movies and soap operas espouse them and suggest that they are really quite harmless.

The movies tell us, "Don't get mad—get even."

The commercials tell us, "Come to my restaurant it's all you can eat."

The soap-operas tell us, "Lust is love and lives aren't destroyed by it."

But it is all a lie. If you try to get even, I can tell you, you will go into a hole and end up in jail. If you eat all you can, you'll eventually be unable to stand. And if you think that lust is love, then never ever expect someone to love you—they will only want to use you.

There are consequences. We reap what we sow. And the consequence of a life out of control is a broken friendship or marriage, addiction to alcohol and drugs, child abandonment and abuse, violence and death. We see it every day on the news.

YOU ARE VALUABLE

The practice of self-control begins when you realize you are worth more than you could possibly know. It begins when you recognize there is one who loves you with an everlasting love. It begins when we recognize that we are out of control and we need to turn our life over to the One who can put the pieces of our life together again. It begins when we understand that the sacred trust we have been given starts with our own life and continues in our care for others.

Yet, so often, people don't believe they are worth that much. They are self-defeating. While we have cared for hundreds of abused children over the years; we have had the occasion to see the homes they have come from, and meet their parents. I am rarely surprised. Invariably, these parents have lived self-destructive lives and these patterns have simply been continued with their children. They haven't understood their worth so how could they possibly understand the value of their child's?

Let me remind you that God had to create a universe so that He would be able to bring you into it. He created this wondrous universe, this amazingly beautiful world just for YOU! He did it so that He would be able to have it ready to receive you when you were to arrive.

Each parent who has expected with love the coming of their child knows this. During the months of waiting and preparing, they paint the baby nursery, search for the right crib, get the right clothing. They buy the best car seats, and toys. The parents do this all in the expectation and preparation of their little one's arrival.

God created this nursery called earth to receive you. He placed things of beauty and quality within that you might be blessed. He gave all the necessary things to be a part of the world that we might have the opportunity to become the person we were created by Him to be. Yet, like any child, sometimes we get ourselves in a mess. And too often we try to solve it ourselves rather then call out to Him for help.

I remember one time when one of my boys decided to open each drawer on his dresser and then walk up it like stairs. Half way up, it fell over on him. But rather than cry out for help, he laid there pinned to the floor. He was afraid that we would be angry at him for doing something foolish and self-destructive—which we were. However, only after we knew that he was not hurt.

We told him that he was more valuable to us and more important to us than any dresser. We showed him that it was dangerous to do such a thing. We told him that he could be hurt and gave him the consequence of having to clean up the mess, after we put the dresser up right, and stay in his room afterward. He learned the lesson and never did it again. But more than all of that, Aaron knew he was loved. And he knew we were there to help him learn the lessons necessary for his growth and would do so in a way that would allow him to be safe. He came to know that there was a reason we wanted him to think before he acted.

FOUR STEPS FOR TEACHING SELF-CONTROL

Teaching self-control is as much about leading by example as it is about teaching. If you lead by example children learn to imitate your calm response to problems. If you show them that when faced with a crisis you can remain calm, they will be able to get the message that this is how someone responds in a crisis.

The second step in teaching self control would be in your own control over not only your emotions but your words. Children learn at their parent's side. If they see their parents swearing and screaming at every frustration, the result is that that will be the way they will respond. Give them other words to use when they are expressing anger like, "I'm angry." "I'm really mad," "I'm frustrated at this." Even the use of the word "ticked" can be used in a way that helps express their frustration. Anger is not wrong. How we express it can be.

For many years I was confused by the fact that nice people don't get angry. The fact is that that view of anger is as self-destructive as a person who is continually angry. Anger is an emotion that God gave us. Anger is not wrong. How we express it can be. Don't deny the child's right to be angry. Just teach them the appropriate way to express it without violence.

Help your child to look for the signs that illustrate they are becoming angry and feeling anger. Help them to easily see and feel the things that cause them to become angry, then help them learn other ways of dealing with those situations, or avoiding them, until they are able to develop the coping mechanism needed to deal with their anger appropriately.

Countless experts have told people to teach their children to actually count to 10 before responding. This doesn't necessarily work in all situations, but it may give the child enough of a pause to gain control of their emotions. It may also help the parent.

I am reminded of a father who was saying as he is watching his child have a tantrum, screaming and yelling and knocking things down in a grocery store. He was heard saying, "Stanley, now calm down. Stanley, don't scream. Stanley don't hit."

A bystander said, "Mister stop telling Stanley to calm down and stop screaming and pick him up."

The father said, "That is not Stanley that is Jimmy, I'm Stanley." We all need to take a moment to pause before responding to anger to any given situation.

SECTION II

The Essential Lessons

Affirmation of life is the spiritual act by which man ceases to live unreflectively and begins to devote himself to his life with reverence in order to raise it to its true value.
~ Albert Schweitzer

The essential lessons of life are the very virtues of a sustainable life. To a society that could very well be called "Generation Stress", the lessons in this section offer the possibility of affirming life and enhancing it.

The widening world tension that was set in motion after the terrorist attacks in New York and Washington on September 11th and the ongoing conflict in Iraq and Afghanistan, and the later terrorist attacks on the Subway and bus transit systems in London England in July of 2005, only deepened the need for these essential lessons.

These lessons are rooted in the core virtues that have been at the heart of every value system of every culture on earth. They are the universal language of character that make possible the integration of spirituality into everyday life.

THE FOG SYNDROME: FATIGUE, OVERWORK, AND GUILT

Most people today live in a FOG. They exist in fatigue due to overwork and guilt. They are driven to distraction by confusion, the cruelty of others and discouragement due to the lack of vision and the motivation to accomplish it. People have to deal with too much work, not enough time to accomplish it, putting up with overbearing bosses and unrealistic expectations of others, downsizing, rightsizing, and outsourcing; the constant shrill of cell-phones and incessant irritation of emails. Without emotional and spiritual resources necessary to cope, the FOG descends. The FOG takes over our minds and takes hold of our spirits and as a result we are left with a chronic lack of motivation that is mixed with depression and anxiety. We are left to run on fumes lacking even the energy to do the things we truly love and enjoy. It is then that guilt takes over because we sense that we have failed to become the fully realized human beings we were meant and desired to be.

The essential lessons offer the knowledge and tools necessary for coping in the world in which we live. These lessons offer us the hope and indeed the promise of a life full and fulfilled when lived.

5

Life Is Confusing—Develop Your Faith

It is always interesting how people react when the subject of faith appears. While I was helping in my daughter's kindergarten class a few years ago, I was introduced to an elderly gentleman who was also helping. He spent his time in the arts and crafts department where he fancied himself an artist.

I was introduced by his daughter (one of the teachers) as a minister and a parent of one of her students. His response was, "Oh, so you're a minister. I don't believe in God. I am like the little girl who when asked about faith said, 'Faith is believing in something that you know is not true.'" He then laughed and turned to leave.

I then said, "Well, you must be a rotten artist."

He turned with a flash of anger and almost shouted, "How dare you! What do you mean?"

I'm always surprised at the offence and indignation of a person who themselves have thought nothing of being ignorant. I responded, "You must be a rotten artist, because any great artist, poet, musician, or scientist believes in what they can't see. A scientist begins with a belief that something is true and steps out in faith and tests that belief. A musician creates majestic and magnificent music that can neither be heard nor seen until written and played; the poet and artist puts paint and pen to page to create something from nothing. Seeing is not believing. Believing is seeing. Since you don't understand this, you are not an artist; and if you are, you are a mediocre paint-by-numbers one at best."

I'm nobody's fool. I know people view faith as foolish and a crutch. They say to me, "But John, you are a minister; you don't live in the real world." What most people don't understand is that I see more of the real world in a week then most people see in a life time. I have cut more people down from their rafters after they have committed suicide; held the hands of more people who were dying of AIDS, and then stood at their grave while comforting their partner and parents; cared for children so malnourished that they have looked like they have been brought to us from a drought in Ethiopia; nursed more severely abused children with broken arms, cracked skulls, and cigarette burns back to health than anyone could possibly imagine. And I can say without a doubt in my mind that faith matters. I also can say without a doubt that everyone lives by faith; the only question is, is it a faith to live by? Is it one that nourishes their spirit and elevates their souls?

Generally there are five ways people respond to the virtue of faith. They either ***ignore it*** believing it doesn't apply to them. They believe it has no relevance to their daily life. Or they ***misunderstand it***. They are like the elderly gentleman who perceived himself as an artist. They just can't get their head around it. Or they ***discount*** its value to everyday life. Or they ***rebel against*** it or they ***explore*** it.

Though skeptical, many philosophers and thinkers still speak of the spirit. Johann Wolfgang von Goethe said, "I am fully convinced that the soul is indestructible, and that its activity will continue through eternity." And the philosopher Teilhard de Chardin said, "We are not human beings having a spiritual experience. We are spiritual beings having a human experience." There is a longing and need to be satisfied within every human soul. And that is only fulfilled through faith.

Faith is the one virtue that can truly give us the necessary strength to face the most difficult of life's storms. I was reminded again of this after caring for a little African-American girl name Jaylyn. She came to our home and remained for six months. She was found in a women's shelter, malnourished, with a woman suffering with mental health problems. They assumed that Jaylyn was her daughter and placed her in our care until the women could be stabilized.

Without anyone's knowledge in Canada there was a search happening for a child who was abducted from Florida by a women with mental health problems. Days turned to weeks, weeks to months and soon the search was called off. Everyone urged the family to give up. They refused. Their church held prayer vigils, fasts and fundraisings to continue the search. They pressured the officials to go beyond their own state in the search by at least notifying other states. In a last ditch effort they expanded their search into Mexico and Canada.

During this time the church and the family continued to hope and believe not willing to give up until they received an answer one way or the other. They prayed specifically for three things with the family. The first thing that they prayed for was that Jaylyn would be found alive; secondly, they prayed that she would be found in a home with children, and finally that that family would be Christian. They knew that most children abducted by someone other than a parent is often dead after 48 hours. However, they believed they would be supported by their faith no matter where she was.

When Jaylyn, who was in my home, was found to be that missing little girl and all three of their prayers were realized, and she was returned home, there was a great celebration.

You could call this a coincidence if you want. But I call it an answer to prayer and an affirmation of faith. The cynics would say, what about the children that are not found alive or cared for. It is a good question. Faith remains even for them a place of refuge and strength, a very present help in trouble.

Others might ask, "How can you believe in a God who would create a world like this where children are abused and Who hasn't done anything about it?" I respond by saying, "God has done something about it. He created you and me. I know what I'm doing about it. Now, what are you going to do?"

FAITH MATTERS

Philip Yancey said, "Faith is trusting in advance what will only make sense in reverse." Every parent who loves their child understands the faith that these little ones put in them. They trust in advance your advice, but often only understand it later. Sometimes they don't even trust it now. They wish to rebel or reject it. However, every parent, when questioned by even their youngest child, tells them what they want to know in as simplistic a way as possible so that they can understand; but often, they still don't. They say, "But why? Why can't I go outside at night alone? I'm a big girl now. I'm four!"

And we say if we are a good parent, "I know you are a big girl now. But even big girls shouldn't go out at night alone. They can get hurt." A four year old doesn't understand all the dangers. They have to trust you because they don't have the wisdom and experience that you have. They don't have the perspective of an adult. From the parent's vantage point it is simply a logical response—four year olds don't go out at night alone. From a child's vantage point it is constraining their freedom—and foolish.

FAITH BRINGS LIFE INTO FOCUS

For people who have faith trusting in a God who has a heavenly perspective and vantage point is not foolish, but wise. Life truly can be confusing. Faith brings clarity to life.

I remember before I needed glasses going to a movie and becoming angry because the movie was blurry. I complained to the manager and asked if he might try to get the person running the film to get it into focus. The manager checked and said that there was no problem. I finished watching the film with little enjoyment and left to go home. I then noticed for the first time that many of the signs in the distance were also very blurry. The eye doctor had little trouble to tell me I needed glasses.

When I put them on everything became crystal clear again. Faith is like that. It is the glasses one puts on to bring clarity to life's blurred vision. Faith brings life into focus.

PUZZLE OF LIFE

I have often described life as a child's picture puzzle box. On the box is a beautiful picture of what the puzzle will be like when it is finish. However, when you remove the cover of the box the pieces in it are just a jumble, a disorganized mess. Like so many others, I needed help to put the pieces of life's puzzle together. I would often want to give up in frustration rather than ask for help. At one point in my life I realized that my life and many others lives are just like that. They look good on the outside but underneath it is just a mess of disorganized pieces. I knew that I needed help sorting everything out and bringing them back together again if I was to live my life in its best way possible. Everyone needs that help.

Jesus put the pieces of the puzzle of my life together again. When I finally got to a point where I knew my life was unmanageable, I turned my life over to Him and committed my life to Him as my Lord and Savior. The moment that I did my life changed forever. The pieces of the puzzle began to find their places more easily and life became brighter, better, and more beautiful. I'm not saying that I have it all together. But the picture is becoming clearer day by day.

Even after committing my life to Christ, I have to admit that there have been many times when I have still made a mess of things, and had to turn again to the Lord for help to reset pieces of my life back into place before I could continue. However, I don't know what I would have done without that faith in One who is able to do what I am unable to do for myself—or by myself.

I know that many people will have problems with this. I know that there are those who have a different point of view than me, and I am not trying to push my faith on anyone. And I know that there will be those who will feel ambivalent toward my saying this. However, I sincerely believe that faith does matter, and that faith does put life into perspective and faith is a key virtue of life that brings forth its meaning and purpose.

Faith is not just a state of mind, but a course of activity. It is not just something that is meant to be possessed but something meant to be practiced. So many of us are hungry for a real spirituality, but have no appetite for religion.

People say to me after discovering that I am a minister, "Oh well, I'm not religious." Or they say, "I do not believe in religion." To which I respond to their shock and confusion, "Neither am I. I don't believe in religion and I am not religious." Once they pick up their chin and stop tripping on their tongue I continue, "I don't believe in religion because my faith isn't about religion it is about a relationship. It is about the vertical relationship with God, and the horizontal relationship with people."

The problem comes when people only focus on one or the other. To have a deeply profound faith, one with deep spiritual roots that produce relevant fruit in your life, you have to have both the vertical and the horizontal relationship. I recall hearing, "That some believers are so heavenly minded that they are no earthly good." However, I also have come to the conclusion that there are others that are so earthly minded that they have no energy to do any good. The fruit that is produced by your faith's spiritual root will either be full and sweet or small and bitter. It depends on how you practice that faith and put it into action.

FAITH IS NOT SEDATE

Faith is not meant to be sedate. It is meant to be fully engaged and active. It is a faith that works. It is meant to impact life in very practical and important ways.

On a Friday night, and the theater was packed for a performance of Tennessee William's *The Night of the Iguana,* starring the notable actress Dorothy McGuire. Just before the curtain was about to rise, a woman in the audience—an overweight, middle-aged woman in a blue print dress—startled the audience by suddenly shouting, "Start the show! Start the show! I want to see Dorothy McGuire! I love Dorothy McGuire!" People sitting next to her quickly moved out of their seats, not wanting to be associated with this madwoman. Ushers and the house manager tried to reason with the woman. Then they reached for her, but she pulled back and continued to shout, "I want to see Dorothy McGuire! Start the show!"

After a moment of shocked silence, the people in the audience decided they had a maniac in their midst and began to get ugly, booing the woman and laughing derisively. Somebody shouted, "Listen you old bag—get out!"

"Throw her out. Start the show!" somebody else yelled.

The woman turned to the shouters, "All I want to see is Dorothy McGuire," she said, "and then I will leave." more laughing and booing—things were edging toward chaos.

Suddenly from behind the curtains, Miss McGuire appeared.

She crossed the stage to the place where the woman was sitting and, with remarkable poise and grace, and kindness, extended her hand toward her. Quietly, willingly, the woman took her hand, and Miss McGuire led her gently toward the exit. As they reached the edge of the auditorium, Miss McGuire paused, turned toward the audience, and said, "I would like to introduce you to a fellow human being."

The audience was stilled, their shouts and taunts silenced by Miss McGuire's compassion, and by the recognition of what they had done. They should have known better. They did know, instead they chose in their mob-like demeanor to act badly.

An old Latin proverb, *"Corruptio optimi pessima"* means, "The worst corruption is the corruption of the best."

FAITH IS NOT PREJUDICED

True faith is not prejudiced. It shows no partiality, no favoritism to one group over another. I was reminded again of how important this is whenever I care for a child from another culture. The fact is we are all human beings. However, so many people focus on what is different about us rather than what we have in common. That is why the scriptures say, "My beloved brothers and sisters, do not hold your faith in our glorious Lord Jesus Christ with an attitude of personal favoritism. For if a man comes into your assembly with a gold ring and dressed in fine cloths, and there also comes in a poor man in dirty cloths, and you pay special attention to the one who is wearing the fine cloths…have you not made distinctions among yourselves, and become judges with evil motives?"[15]

Being partial or prejudiced is in total conflict with our understanding of the Christian faith. If we are children of God, then ought we not to act like it? In the sacred scriptures we also read, "How blessed is he who considers the helpless; the Lord will deliver him in a day of trouble."[16] And again, we are warned? "He who mocks the poor reproaches his Maker."[17]

There is no room for prejudice within Christianity. Yet when prejudice is found we also find a dead faith—and a false witness.

People can be so cruel and children, at times, especially cruel. A few years ago, my children, Nathanael, Aaron and Tabitha, were at a Vacation Bible School. Nathanael and Aaron were playing with Tabitha and their new friends after it was over. A young boy came up to Nathanael and asked, as he pointed to Tabitha, "Who is that?"

He said, "She is my sister."

The boy said, "She's black, she is not your sister."

Nathanael said, "Yes, she is."

Tabitha, then stuck her head out from behind her brother's protective back and said, "I'm not black, I'm caramel. And you are not white you are peach. I know my colors. I'm four years old now."

But the boy yelled, "She is not", and punched Nathanael. I want to tell you; I wanted to find that boy. I don't know what made me angrier, the fact that this prejudice still remains in the church and someone was teaching this child to be prejudiced, or that it got violent. No one is born prejudiced. They have to be taught to be prejudiced.

That is why we have to be so careful, how we treat one another. W.B. Yeats expressed it this way;

Had I the heaven's embroidered cloths
Enwrought with golden and silver light,
The blue and the dim and the dark cloths
Of night and light and half light,
I would spread the cloths under your feet:
But I, being poor, have only my dreams;

I have spread my dreams under your feet;
Tread softly because you tread on my dreams.

People can be so cruel until they learn to live differently. Yet this partiality—this cruelty comes in all sorts of ways. A nine-year-old named Philip was in a Sunday School class of eight-year-olds. The other children did not welcome Philip and often made fun of him, not because he was older, but because he was "different." Phillip suffered from Down's syndrome with its physical characteristics and slow responses. One Sunday, the teacher gave each child a plastic egg that pulls apart in the middle. She instructed her students to go outdoors, find a symbol of "new life" and place it within the egg. The children eagerly complied. Afterwards, the teacher opened each egg, giving the children an opportunity to see what the other students had found. One placed a pretty flower in the egg. The children showed their approval. Another egg revealed a tiny butterfly. Everyone agreed that it was beautiful. Finally, the teacher opened the last egg, and it was empty. "That's stupid," said one of the little boys in the class. Then the teacher felt a tug on his shirt. It was Phillip. Looking up he said, "That's mine. I did it. I have new life because the tomb is empty."

A hush fell over the class. From that time forward, Phillip became a part of the group. Whatever had made him different was never mentioned again.

That summer, Phillip died. In his own way, he had been poor in this world, but *rich in faith.* God chose him to teach others the meaning of the resurrection and of life. At his funeral, nine 8-year-old boys and girls filed past his casket, each placing an empty plastic egg alongside the flowers already there.

These children learned to be more willing to accept people who are different. If only everyone could do that.

FAITH IS PRACTICAL

The test of real faith is that it is not partial, and that it is practical. The scripture says, "If a brother or sister is without clothing and in need of daily food, and one of you says to them, "Go in peace, be warmed and be filled," and yet you do not give them what is necessary for their body, what use it that?"[18]

Real faith has hands and feet on it. James said that we are not to be just hearers of the word but doers of it. Faith is meant to be practical.

A very interesting incident took place at the University of California at Berkeley when some maintenance men entered a storage room. They found a stack of pamphlets called *Control of Termites*. Then discovered the entire stacks of pamphlets had been eaten through by the subject of the books. The university knew how to solve the problem of termites, but they didn't act on the knowledge they had.

That's the way it is all too often. Isn't it? We know what the Scriptures say and what the "Golden Rule" is and we know what we ought to do. However, we fail to act on that knowledge.

Marian Anderson is well known as an outstanding opera star. Toscanini told her that she had the finest voice of the century. She was invited to the White House to give a private concert for the Roosevelts and the King and Queen of England. Her hometown of Philadelphia awarded her the Bok Award as the person who had done the most for the city. The award was named after a wealthy Philadelphia financier, Edward Bok and presented each year to the person who was considered to be the most outstanding Philadelphian of the year.

On that occasion, Marion Anderson stood beneath the Lincoln statue and sang for a crowd of 75,000 including most of the high-ranking leaders of government. However when asked by a newspaper reporter to name the greatest moment in her life, she referred to none of those outstanding events. Instead, she said the greatest moment of her life was the day she went home and told her mother she wouldn't have to do other people's washing anymore, that she could provide for her mother.

FAITH IS PROFITABLE

Faith must make a difference. Faith expresses itself in love. The New English Bible says: "Faith is active in love." I believe that when God comes to judge us, the question is not going to be whether we were obedient to the law. The question is going to be whether we have turned to God in faith and then turn to the world around us and acted on that faith in a way that made a difference.

A minister was talking to a professing Christian and asked him if he was active in a local church. The man responded, "No, but the dying thief on the cross wasn't active in any church and yet he was still accepted." The minister then asked if he was acting on that faith by doing good things. The man responded, "The dying thief on the cross didn't do anything good so why should I and he still made it to heaven." The minister then asked if he had served the God by at least helping others. The man responded, "No, but the dying thief didn't either, and Christ still received him."

The minister then commented: "The only difference between you and the dying thief is that he was dying in his belief, and you are dead in yours." Real faith is active.

The young boy came to us one weekend near Christmas. He was as emotionally withdrawn, his eyes sunken in his head. His name was Liam. He was wearing ragged clothes and worn out running shoes. When I knelt down to take his hand he cowered and hid behind the police officer's leg; as tears streamed from his eyes. He was small, and emaciated. I handed him a teddy bear and he sheepishly stuck out his hand to receive it and with the other wrapped his little fingers around one of mine.

Over the course of the evening and weekend he began to come out of his shell. He seemed to be fascinated with the Crèche and the baby Jesus in particular. I asked Liam if he knew the Christmas story of the birth of Jesus and he did. He said, "I know things, I am four you know."

"Yes dear, I know." I said.

He would play for what seemed like hours with all the camels, sheep and wisemen and shepherds and when he left the Crèche he would take the baby Jesus with him in his pocket and skipping a little as he went to play elsewhere. Returning later he'd place the baby Jesus in the straw and play again with the manger. He seemed to brighten when he played there and so we let him.

When it came time for Liam to leave, there were more tears, but with the tears and hugs came "I love you." He clutched his teddy bear close walking hand in hand with us in his new clothes and Christmas toys to the car and the worker who would be taking him away. As we looked at him, he seemed less withdrawn and perhaps a little taller than he had been when he came. But of course that couldn't be. He had been with us only a week. Yet, obviously something had changed.

A day or so later one of the children noticed that the baby Jesus was nowhere to be found. He was not in the Crèche. We looked high and low but could not find him. It was then that Tabitha said, "I think Liam took Jesus with him."

"That's okay." I said. "If Liam took Jesus with him, he obviously needed him." I have always hoped he had.

6

Life Can Be Disheartening—So Develop Your Optimism

People of faith are prisoners of hope.
~ Archbishop Desmond Tutu

I was asked by a reporter for the National Post after my wife Liane and I received the Governor General's Meritorious Service Medal when after seeing so much violence, inhumanity and abuse done to so many vulnerable innocents, if we have ever become jaded or cynical. I replied, "It certainly would be easy to become jaded or cynical about a system that continually sends children to the very people who abuse them, only to have them return to us or others to mend their broken bones and shattered spirits. We haven't become cynical or jaded because we act on the hope that we have, what is rooted in our faith, that one day things will change; and until they do, we have chosen to become the change we want to see in the world."

Hope is vitally important in life. Faith is about believing that change can happen. It is about recognizing that life can be disheartening and choosing not to be discouraged by it. Hope is about acting on faith. Hope is the stuff of faith. Whenever people have brought about change in the world it has been because they believed it could happen, and they held onto the hope that it would happen. "Change always begins with some people making decisions based in hope, and then staking their lives on those decisions."[19] However, when people loose hope they often give up on life.

I remember responding to a person who came to my home asking for money. I had just been newly ordained and settled as the new minister in a small village in a farming community. The village had a population of approximately 100 women, men and children, and another 100 more from the outlying area. I came to know, during that time, almost all the people who were on welfare.

What was particularly interesting was a person and his family who were actually receiving more money on welfare and the bit of work he did "under the table" than I was making at the time as a new minister. At that time I was supporting my wife who was pregnant and two daughters. Yet, he had given up all hope of ever overcoming his situation and rebuilding his life when he came to me for help.

I brought him food for his family from my cupboards and fridge and a can of coffee. We sat and spent some time talking. I soon found that he was illiterate and many—if not all—of the people in his family and community were as well. I encouraged him to learn how to read and told him I would take the time and set up a class to teach him and his family and anyone else who wanted to learn to read. He didn't believe that it would make any difference to his situation. And he wanted nothing to do with it. He had given up any hope of changing his lot in life. He came from a long line of welfare recipients and lived in a shanty town they called Keelerville in a makeshift house with dirt floors and no running water. He, his family and friends, had slapped this shack up years before on land that wasn't theirs. They were squatters on public land like many from his community.

Over the years the generals and with others from that community, all had given up hope of ever changing their life situation. Many refused to believe that there was a better life for them.

I began to think about what difference there was between us. He was a person loved by God even if he thought that he wasn't valued by God or by others. I cared for him and his community and wanted desperately to see a better life for them as I battled against their lack of hope. They had no hope. While I was sustained by my faith and compelled by hope to make a difference in my life, family, community and world. He had long ago given up trying to make a difference in his life and didn't see the need to change anything for his children. He saw, only the continuing legacy of being on welfare for generations to come. He asked if I knew what the new welfare regulations were so that he would know what new thing he needed to do to convince the social workers to keep him and his family on welfare. He looked at me with a vacant gaze when I suggested that a better way of living was possible.

I understood what it was like to be broke. As I look back at my family I am convinced that I came from a family that would be today considered the working poor. I remember overhearing the strained hushed words of my mother as she spoke with fear in her voice to my father one night as I rubbed my eyes awake, about her panic of not being able to make the rent and pay the bills. The next day I got a job and began buying my own things to lessen their burden. Later, I discovered that I was making more money per hour on my first full-time job than my father did after a life time of working. I know what it is like to be broke; but I never thought of myself as poor and nor did my family. They always looked with hope for better days. And those days did arrive. I have had times when I thought I was down, but I never believed I was out. My family had instilled in me a firm faith and definite hope for a brighter future.

I realized that being broke is about having no money; being poor is about having no hope. No one is ever poor if they have hope. You may be down, but you do not have to be out. Hope is truly important to life.

A powerful story that illustrates the importance of hope was when Desmond Tutu of South Africa spoke at St. George's Cathedral in Cape Town. The Nobel Peace Prize winner and Anglican Cleric chose to preach there because a political rally had just been cancelled by the white government, so Bishop Tutu called for a worship service instead. The authorities came and showed their power seeking to frighten those who were speaking out again Apartheid. The riot police and armed soldiers massed outside the church, and inside along the walls stood the police openly taping and recording every word. When Tutu rose to speak, the atmosphere was tense. He confidently proclaimed that the evil and oppression of the system of Apartheid cannot prevail. At that moment, the South African archbishop was probably one of the few people on the planet who actually believed that. He pointed his finger right at the police who were recording his words. "You may be powerful, indeed very powerful, but you are not God! And the God who we serve," said Tutu, "cannot be mocked! You have already lost!" the diminutive preacher thundered. Then he stepped out from behind the pulpit and his voice softened, flashing that signature smile. "So, since they have already lost," he said, "we are inviting you to come and join the winning side!" The whole place erupted, the police seemed to scurry out, and the congregation rose up in triumphal dance.[20]

Hope is the one thing that helps you to hold on when others think all is lost and want you to let go and give up.

HOPE IS NOT OPTIMISM

The difference between hope and optimism is that optimism very often can change depending on the circumstances. If things are going well we are optimistic, if things are going badly, we are pessimistic. Hope, on the other hand, is rooted in something far deeper. It is rooted in a faith that does not change. The foundation of faith allows us to have the stability to weather the storms, tides and turbulence of life. Hope is the compass that guides us through those storms.

Hope, unlike faith or love, is often seen to be elusive and therefore irrelevant. It is nothing of the sort. We can speak of works of faith and works of love, but we cannot do so with regard to hope. Not being able to do so does not make it irrelevant. Rather, hope is that which enables us to caste our vision into the future and while there perceive the pathway to a greater good for ourselves, our family, community and world. After which, hope then takes our hand and leads us to that greater good and brighter future.

HOPE GIVES BIRTH TO OPTIMISM

The old adage "hope springs eternal" is true. Hope is the positive virtue that every person must have. Hope makes it possible to endure incredible obstacles with optimism and a positive outlook. In a world such as ours where there is such inhumanity to other human beings this is something that we must all hold onto.

Each day when we turn on our televisions, read newspapers and listen to radio we are engulfed by images of starving, dying people on the streets of Calcutta; racial inhumanity and hostility in various parts of Africa; terrorist bombings, and wars in Iraq, and Afghanistan; murders and violence on the streets of Canada and America. Overwhelmed and besieged, many of us simply put down the paper, turn off the TV, and the radio to soothe our minds and comfort our souls. We are tempted to think that it is hopeless and just give up.

What is it about hope that allows people to endure such unspeakable torment and yet hold out for that better day? St. Thomas Aquinas assures, "The object of hope is a future good, difficult but possible to obtain" Even though the future good may be difficult to attain, it doesn't mean it is not worthwhile to strive to attain it. That takes hope.

PROFILES IN HOPE

What do people like Nelson Mandela, Martin Luther King Jr., Desmond Tutu, Billy Graham, Pope John Paul II, Mother Teresa, Maya Angelou, and Oprah Winfrey have in common? They are all people of hope. They offer us a profile of hope in action.

WORDS OF HOPE

I offer you words of hope that have comforted and encouraged me over the years.

Jeremiah 29:11	*(NIV)* "For I know the plans I have for you," declares the Lord, "plans to prosper you and not to harm you, plans to give you hope and a future."
Psalm 42:5	*(NIV)* "Why are you downcast, O my soul? Why so disturbed within me? Put your hope in God…"
Psalm 130:7	*(NIV)* "Put your hope in the Lord, for with the Lord is unfailing love and with him is full redemption."
Jeremiah 17:7	*(NIV)* "Blessed is the man who trusts in the Lord, and whose hope is the Lord."
Psalm 62:5-8	*(NIV)* "Find rest, O my soul, in God alone; my hope comes from Him. He alone is my rock and my salvation; he is my fortress, I will not be shaken. My salvation and my honor depend on God; he is my mighty rock, my refuge. Trust in him at all times, O people; pour out your hearts to him, for God is our refuge."

Woodrow Kroll wrote the following poem that I have often returned to in times of difficulty.

Start Over

When you've trusted Jesus and walked His way,
When you've felt His hand lead you day by day,
But your steps now take you another way…Start over.
When you've made your plans and they've gone awry,
When you've tried your best till there is no more try,
When you've failed yourself and you don't know why…
Start over.
When you've told your friends what you plan to do,
When you've trusted them, but they didn't come through,
Now you are all alone and it's up to you…Start over.
When you failed your kids, and they're grown and gone,
When you've done your best but it turned out wrong,
And now your grandchildren have come along…Start over
When you've prayed to God so you'll know His will,
When you've prayed and prayed but you don't know still,
When you want to stop 'cause you've had your fill…Start over.
When you think you're finished and want to quit,
When you've bottomed out in life's deepest pit,
When you've tried to get out of it…Start over.
When the year's been long and successes few,
When December comes you're feeling blue,
God gives a January just so you…Start over.
Starting over means victories won.
Starting over means a race well run.
Starting over means the Lord's…"Well done!"[21]

7

Life Can Be Cruel—Decide to Be Kind

All virtue is summed up in dealing justly.
~ Aristotle

Samuel Johnson feels, "Kindness is within our powers, fondness is not." That could be a liberating sentence. We sometimes feel we have an obligation to like everybody and, when we can't manage it, we grow discouraged and feel guilty. But fondness is not within our powers. Kindness is, however, and we know that we can be kind even to people we don't like. And then the surprise! What begins in kindness often leads to fondness. When we treat people right, we begin to feel right about them. We have all known people who are mean and cruel. The great spiritual lesson I learned was that in the face of cruelty choose kindness. Choose to be a blessing.

Whenever I'm disappointed with things, I sometimes think about little Jamie Scott. Jamie was trying out for a part in a school play. His mother had told a friend that he had his heart set on being in it, though she feared he might not be chosen. On the day the parts were announced, her friend went with the mother to collect him after school. Jamie rushed up to her, eyes shining with pride and excitement. "Guess what, Mum," he shouted.

She, surprised asked, "What? Did you get the part!"

"Nope. Better! I've been chosen to clap and cheer!" He had been chosen to be a benediction. We all need people to be for us those who would clap and cheer.[22] We all need cheerleaders. We all need people who are blessings.

Most of the children that come into our home have never had someone to be their cheerleader. No one to encourage them with words of praise and expressions of love and approval.

Everyone needs encouragement. *Everyone!*

As a parent to 1000 children I have found that encouragement is often the key that unlocks the child's hidden potential. It doesn't take much to discover a little thing about a child that with a small push of encouragement will cause them to blossom. It may be something simple like saying to a little girl that she colored a picture beautifully, or sang sweetly, or shared appropriately, that will cause the child to want to do it again. With each encouraging word or look the child comes further out of their shell and will venture into areas of study or play, or appropriate behaviors they might never have tried if it were not for a bit of encouragement.

This was another lesson I learned from the children. Everyone needs encouragement, because life can be very discouraging at times. However, when you have a cheerleader in your corner it makes all the differences. Choose to be a cheerleader. Choose to be a blessing.

A THANKFUL HEART

Being a blessing involves a thankful heart. To be thankful or grateful is to recognize the blessings one has received. Hugh Kingswell, one of Malcolm Muggeridges close friends, said, "Friends are God's apology for relatives." Isn't that true? We can't choose our relatives, but we can choose our friends. Thank God for that. As I see the families of some of the little children we have cared for, I pray that they will find people who they can rely on; people who will be a blessing to them.

Being thankful is about recognizing the gifts and blessings that have entered your life and showing appreciation by acting in the same manner toward others. We are blessed so that we can be a blessing.

However, sometimes we forget this and become like the man who met an acquaintance when he was out walking his pig with a peg leg. The man when they met, asked, "What are you doing with that pig?"

The man with the pig said, "You don't understand this is a great pig. This pig saved my daughter's life. Two weeks ago, we were swimming and my daughter nearly drowned. This pig ran into the water, swam up to her and pulled her to safety. This is a great pig. And this week, we were sleeping, and the pig smelt smoke and woke us all up. It saved our whole family and house. This is a great pig!"

"Wow, but what is with the peg leg?"

"You've got to understand. You don't eat a pig like this all at once."

You don't eat a pig like this at all unless you are an ungrateful pig yourself. The problem of course is we don't think things through. If we would think more, we might give thanks more. Did you know that the root word for "thank" is the same for think? Perhaps, if we think more we would thank more.

Often the reason we don't give thanks, is because we get caught up in the problems and pressures of our life. We ask, "Why should I give thanks? After all, look at what is happening to me? No one should expect me to thank God after all I've been through." As a result of that negative thinking we hold on to our burdens and become a burden to ourselves and to others. Some give all sorts of reasons why they become bitter. However, does being bitter make you better?

A few years ago at the Seattle Special Olympics, nine contestants, all physically or mentally disabled, assembled at the starting line for the 100 yard dash. At the gun they all started out, not exactly in a dash, but with the relish to run the race to the finish and win.

All, that is, except one boy who stumbled on the asphalt, tumbled over a couple of times, and began to cry. The other eight heard the boy cry. They slowed down then paused. Then all turned around went back—every one. A girl with Down's Syndrome bent down and kissed him and said, "This will make it better." Then all nine linked arms and walked together to the finish line.

Everyone in the stadium stood, and the cheering went on, and on, and on.

And heaven joined in. They didn't become bitter because of their circumstances, they became better and a blessing.

PAINFUL FACTS

Being a blessing also involves painful facts. If you are going to be a blessing you are going to experience pain. When you are trying to bless people you enter into a relationship with them. And relationships can be painful. Painful because of the *risk of rejection.* Jamie Buckingham tells us, "The truth will make you free, but first it will make you miserable." I agree and every husband should. We know that the truth will make us free, but first it will make us miserable because of our wives asking very dangerous questions. Questions like, "Do you like this dress?" Or, "Do you like my hair-do?" Do they really expect us to tell them the truth? We know that the truth in such a moment may make us free, but the wrong answer might make us miserable.

People don't really want to hear it. "True friends stab you in the front." Why, because they tell you the truth. Friends don't let friends drive drunk. Friends risk rejection, by telling the truth. The truth sometimes hurts.

There was a conductor who had a habit of throwing things when the orchestra didn't play it right. He would often snap at rehearsals, "Beethoven got it right! And you—YOU got it wrong!" He would then throw things. At the end of the concert year, the orchestra gathered to give a gift to their conductor who has told them the truth and helped them attain near perfection. When he opened it, he found two watches one very expensive, and the other one very cheap. Engraved on the inexpensive one were the words. "For rehearsals only!"

Being a blessing is painful because of the risk of rejection but also because of the *reality of loss.* Let me give you another principle. The beginning of a relationship presupposes its end. Situations change, people move on, people die—and if there is love there is loss. It is a clear and painful fact.

George Beverly Shea sang at a Crusade just after his wife Erma had passed away. A friend, Fred Smith, spoke to him afterwards and commented, "Bev, I don't think I have ever heard you sing more beautifully then you just did." It was then that tears welled up in Shea's eyes, "You know what Fred; it is then that I miss Erma the most. It is then that I want to go home and tell her. But I can't" You can only brag to people who love you. When you love someone, you cheerlead them, you encourage them for you want them to have everything that God would provide.

Being a blessing also *costs.* That is another reason people find it hard to be a blessing. It costs. There is a story about a six-year-old girl who became deathly ill suffering from a dreaded disease. To survive, she needed a blood transfusion from someone who had previously conquered the same illness. The situation was complicated by her rare blood type. Her nine-year-old brother qualified as a donor, but everyone was hesitant to ask him since he was just a little boy. Finally they agreed to have the doctor pose the question. The attending physician tactfully asked the boy if he was willing to be brave and donate blood for his sister. Though he didn't understand much about such things, the boy agreed without hesitation: "Sure, I'll give my blood for my sister." He lay down beside his sister and smiled at her as they pricked his arm with the needle. Then he closed his eyes and lay silently on the bed as the pint was taken.

Soon thereafter the physician came in to thank the little fellow. The boy, with quivering lips and tears running down his cheeks, asked, "Doctor, when do I die?" At that moment the doctor realized that the naive little boy thought that by giving his blood, he was also giving up his life. Quickly he reassured the lad that he was not going to die, but amazed at his courage, the doctor asked, "Why were you willing to risk your life for her?" Because she is my sister … and I love her, I love her."

Don't fool yourself. Being a blessing is painful—it costs. However, it is a price worth paying.

A PURPOSEFUL WORK

Being a blessing also involves a purposeful work. Do you know what your purpose is on earth? If not that may be the reason you get so frustrated and angry.

If you want to make your children angry go to Disney World without them. If you want to make them really angry bring back pictures. We did both.

While in Florida to receive my Doctorate at a weekend convocation, Liane and I, on the spur of the moment, took a flight to Disney World. While there I was fascinated to watch as security guards walked with Mickey Mouse, Minnie, Chip and Dale and all the other Disney characters around the park as they greeted people. It puzzled me why they would need a security person so I asked one of the security guards why he was there. The guard said, "People are crazy! Just the other day they attacked one of the Disney Characters and she was thrown into the bush. People are crazy. The Disney Character I was escorting had to leave the area and this gentleman was upset because he didn't get a picture of Minnie with his kid." It's pretty bad, when people are attacking Minnie and Mickey causing a need for protection. People forget they are there to have fun and instead they too often loose their patience and become frustrated.

Why are we so angry? Why do we get so frustrated? Because we have forgotten or perhaps never found out why we are here. As a result, people focus on their problems rather than their purpose.

A missionary from Haiti, had returned home to Florida on

furlough and had told about the horror of Haiti, and someone who had figured that she would stay home after her furlough said, "What are you going to do after the year is up."

She said, "I'm going to go back to hell. That's what I'm going to do. I'm going back to hell, and I'm going to plant some flowers."

That's what we do. We must plant flowers—seeds of blessing—and when they have blossomed we are to show them to each other and experience their beauty and fragrance. That is what it is to be focused on our purpose rather than the problem. That is what it is to be a blessing.

JOYFUL DEMEANOR

When we breathe in the fragrance from the flowers that came forth from our seeds of blessings we experience joy. And that joyful demeanor is like a light that brightens not only our day but the others around us.

A recent study found that adults laugh 15 times a day. You might think that is a lot. However children laugh up to 400 times a day. That was one of the differences that I discovered when those little battered and abused children came into our home. They didn't laugh or smile. Yet, after they lived with us and were encouraged and loved and played, the smiles slowly emerged and then we'd hear them laugh and laugh and laugh.

Why the difference? It is because these children, like we adults, learned to take life seriously. They, like us, got caught up in a life that was unhappy. However, when placed in an environment that allowed them to be children again and not have to be on their guard as adults, they began to experience joy again, or for the first time. Perhaps that is why Jesus said we need to be like little children. Too often we get caught up in ourselves and our problems; like the woman who was so frustrated with her weight that she prayed, "Lord if you can't make me thin, at least make my friends look fat."

The world is filled with people with bad news, long faces, and heavy hearts. Much of today's popular music, speaks of misery, sorrow and despair. Newspapers thrive on tragedies and calamities, lost jobs and horrible accidents. The same can be said of television news. We give primary attention to storms, droughts and blizzards. We are told, "Tomorrow will be partly cloudy with a 20 percent chance of rain," Whatever happened to mostly clear and 80 percent chance of sunshine! Where are those people who can brighten our days and whose joy is infectious? Why don't you be that person? It begins by being a blessing and ends with love and joy.

SECTION III

The Spiritual Lessons

A little girl arrived at midnight clutching tightly a bracelet that she received from her mother. While she stayed in our home, she was never without it. She took it everywhere. However, one morning when she awoke she discovered the bracelet was nowhere to be found. She became frantic. She tore through the house pulling things apart and looking under chairs and cushions to find it. She continued to become increasingly hysterical. I attempted to assure her that we would find it. I asked her why she was so distressed.

She collapsed in tears and said, "When my mother would leave me somewhere I would always ask to wear her bracelet. She thought I liked the bracelet, but that wasn't it at all. I knew I wasn't worth coming back for, but I knew she would come back for her bracelet. I have to find it! Or she will never come back for me." We eventually did find it. We returned to her bedroom to find it tangled in the bedding.

Throughout this, I tried to assure her that she was more valuable then any bracelet, but it wasn't until we found it that she felt secure again.

I have discovered that some people feel they are of no value. They think that they are worthless. As a result they seek that approval or sense of security, significance and satisfaction in things that don't last. Let me assure you of this fact. You are far more valuable to God than anything that you can do or anything you possess.

HAPPINESS

What is it that you are looking for? Some say it is happiness. But, happiness can be an elusive thing. Thomas Jefferson borrowed from Englishman John Locke when he said, "That the fundamental right of every person is life, liberty and the pursuit of happiness." And insofar as we are influenced by both the British and the American culture and values, many feel it is a fundamental right of ours as well in Canada.

Yet, I wonder if our pursuit of it is the problem. How often have you thought, "If only I had that job, or that person in my life, or that car, or that thing, then I would be happy." However, after having it for a time you find that kind of happiness doesn't last.

A man who felt that his life would be complete and he would be completely happy if he could just have a Ferrari. So he saved every penny he could get his hands on. He worked extra hours and then came the day that he bought the Ferrari. It was the proudest day of his life. He drove it, showed it to his friends. He knew it was a bit more than he could afford, and that he would have to stretch to make the payments and insurance, but he thought that would be O.K. On the way home, he went into the corner store for something. When he came out he noticed that someone had scratched the car. He was furious. And from that moment on he began to worry about what else would happen to the car, until finally he stopped driving it all together, leaving it in his driveway. He worried about it all the time. He worried about the payments, and about the problems, and about whether someone may damage it further. What was once his dream had now become his nightmare. He ended the nightmare the logical way by selling the car.

The problem with the pursuit of happiness is that we pursue it through possessions, position, power or privilege. Be wary of these four "Ps". We go from having a game show that asks and answers the question, "Who wants to be a millionaire?" to a game show that asks, "Who wants to marry a multi-millionaire?" And the contestants are shocked to discover it doesn't work out.

The problem with the pursuit of happiness is not just that we pursue it through possessions, position, power or privilege—the problem is that we try to pursue it all at once. Happiness is something that comes as a by-product of a life well lived. It is the surprise in the "Cracker Jack" box or the toy in the middle of the chocolate egg. A life well lived is blessed and sweet. Happiness is something you find in the middle of living it with passion and purpose.

James Dobson tells the story about a woman who gave her son no affection, no love, no discipline, and no training during his early years. Other children had little to do with him, so he was alone most of the time. He became an outcast. Absolutely rejected from his earliest childhood. When he reached his thirteenth year a school psychologist commented that he probably didn't even know the meaning of the word "love." During adolescence, the girls would have nothing to do with him and he continually fought with the boys.

Despite a high IQ, he failed academically, and finally dropped out during his third year of high school. He thought he might find a new acceptance in the Marine Corps, but he continued to have problems even in the Corps. The other Marines laughed at him and he became a center of ridicule. He fought back, resisted authority, and was court-martialed and thrown out of the Marines with an undesirable discharge. So there he was, a young man in his early twenties, absolutely friendless. His life a mess. He wasn't much to look at, either, small and skinny. Hardly a picture of a heroic Marine. His voice had an odd squeak. He had no discernable talent, no skill, no sense of worthiness. He didn't even have a driver's license. He continued to run from his problems. He moved to a foreign country to live. While there, he married a girl who herself had been an illegitimate child. He brought her back to America with him.

Soon after this she began to develop the same contempt for him that everyone else displayed. Together they had two children, but he never had the love or respect of his children. His marriage eventually crumbled. His wife demanded more and more things that he could not provide. Instead of being his ally she became another enemy. She could outfight him, and she learned to bully him. On one occasion, she locked him in the bathroom as punishment. Finally, she forced him to leave.

Not long after this he woke up a strangely different man. He arose, went to the garage, and took down a rifle he had hidden there. He carried it with him to his newly acquired job at a book-storage building. And from a window on the third floor of that building, shortly after noon, November 22, 1963, he sent two bullets crashing into the head of President John Fitzgerald Kennedy.[23]

Dr. James Dobson said, "Lee Harvey Oswald, the rejected, unlovable failure, killed the man who, more than any other man on earth, embodied all the success, beauty, wealth, and family affection which he lacked."

Oswald kept asking three questions: How do I look? How am I doing? How important am I? He based his whole miserable life on appearance, achievement and status. Ironically, he failed every one. "He gained a place in history by demonstrating his hostility," Dobson said. "Yet, the questions he asked are the same questions our society lives or dies by in its pursuit of happiness, How do I look? How am I doing? How important am I?" These are the questions of security, sufficiency, and significance. They speak to the deepest of human needs and to the problem of our pursuit of happiness.

More than ever I am convinced the Beatitudes—the Blessed Lessons—or the Lessons that Bless have the answers to the basic needs of our personal lives. In the words of Jesus we gain an understanding of the practical principles for learning to be human in an inhumane world. In the Beatitudes we learn how to enjoy inner happiness. The Sermon on the Mount does not present the way of riches, but the way of right living.

Warren Wiersbe comments, "...the Sermon on the Mount has both present and future implications...I believe God wants each of His children to live like a king, and the Beatitudes help point the way to that experience."

D. M. Lloyd-Jones M.D. keenly observed: "If you want to have power in your life and to be blessed, go straight to the Sermon on the Mount. Live and practice it and give yourself to it, and as you do so the promised blessings will come...The Sermon is a description of character and not a code of ethics or of morals...but rather a description of what we are meant to be."

Jesus suggested that we can live a life that is blessed, a life that we will live above the chances, changes, and circumstances in life, " ... I came that they might have life and might have it abundantly."[24] The scripture describes this kind of life as one that is filled with "... love, joy, peace, patience, kindness, goodness, faithfulness, gentleness, self-control; against such things there is no law" [25] If you want these things in your life learn the blessed lessons well and you will have them.

Some of the lessons of the Beatitudes will be found in other sections of this book because they are universal lessons; however, the remainder will be found here in the section called *The Spiritual Lessons.*

8

Life Can Be Damaging—Be A Blessing

"Blessed are the poor in spirit, for theirs is the kingdom of heaven.... Blessed are those who are persecuted for righteousness sake, for theirs is the kingdom of heaven."

When Liane and I began our work as an emergency home for crack and heroin addicted, abandoned, abused infants and toddlers from birth to five years of age, we were not looking for honors or notoriety. In fact, for nearly 20 years we seldom spoke of what we did. The only people aware of the work were the people in the congregations I served during that time. It was not thought of as significant by us or others. It was simply something that we did and others knew we did. It was taken for granted that each Sunday when we arrived for the service we might have a few extra children with us. They knew that we would keep the Sunday school in business.

It wasn't until the Empire Club of Canada heard of our work and the Lieutenant Governor of Ontario The Honourable Hilary Weston awarded us with the Humanitarian of the Year award that our work came to light. Even then, Liane would have preferred that we be left in obscurity.

It was the result of this award that I began to be asked to visit various places and tell the stories, and the lessons I learned and speak about the changes that I saw that were necessary to the family and criminal laws of our land. As a child protection advocate it became important that the stories got out, so that I could connect with the hearts of the people to help them open their homes to more love and compassion and perhaps to even one of these little children that we cared for.

It was for that reason that I wrote, *How I Became a Father to 1000 Children and the Lessons Learned.* I wanted people to experience the joy and happiness that we have known when we have seen a child, once shattered due to abuse, become strong, healthy and joyful again even for the first time. I wanted people to step up and be counted. I wanted people to understand that they could make a difference here and realize their importance in a very real way. I wanted them to know that life is blessed, and that they could be a blessing, and in doing so, experience true happiness.

LIVE HUMBLY

Too often we equate happiness with wealth rather than life itself. We often fail to see that the sacred has significance to life. And that it is there, where we will find true happiness filled with joy, peace and contentment. True blessedness is found, in the way of those who are poor in spirit and those who are persecuted for what is right. However, we would rather convince ourselves that the opposite is true. We would rather believe that a truly blessed life is found with the lifestyles of the rich and famous. Yet, in our better moments we, and they, honor those who live truly blessed lives—like Nelson Mandela, Rosa Park and Mother Teresa who have changed the world.

Nelson Mandela, who was a leading opponent of South African Apartheid during the early 1960s, found himself arrested in 1962 and imprisoned for twenty-seven years before his release in 1989. He endured persecution for standing up for what is right and against what is wrong. And rather than exacting revenge on those who imprisoned him when he was released, he simply and humbly led the nation of South Africa into a peaceful transitional government seeking not revenge but justice. It is no wonder that he has been honored the world over.

Often those who are honored do not think that they deserve the honor. They do not think that they have done anything special or significant. They have simply done what was necessary at the right time because it was the correct thing to do.

Rosa Park, as a black southerner, simply refused to give up her seat on a bus for a white person. In that simple act of humble defiance which honored her own human dignity she changed the United States of America. It was a simple act. Yet the ramifications became most profound affecting millions of lives.

She and Nelson Mandela understood that they were the blessed of God and were meant to be a blessing. Do you? You're the blessed of God. You are meant to be a blessing. Rosa Park understood that she was valued by God. She understood she was equal to a white person in the sight of God and had as much right to the seat as anyone else, black or white. She honored her human dignity with humbleness and grace.

When I speak of you being the blessed of God, I mean that

you are at the core of your being a person of dignity, honor and nobility. As a child of God you are an heir of His kingdom and honor. You are worthy of being treated with respect simply by virtue of your birth and are expected to treat others with that same respect and esteem.

Violence and abuse against others—whether that be toward men, women, children or other cultures—is at its core a lack of respect and esteem for one's self and for that other person's inalienable right as a human being to be treated with dignity. To degrade another person is to demean yourself for you are no different than them.

When you grasp your inalienable right to have and feel human dignity, like Rosa Park and Nelson Mandela and Mother Teresa, you begin to live differently. You begin to refuse to be treated disrespectfully. You begin to honor your own human dignity.

One of the most difficult things we have to teach the children who come into our home is that they are worthy of love. They have been told for so long that they are bad and evil and deserve to be treated harshly, violently and without dignity. They begin to believe it and expected and do things to receive the humiliation. At times it takes months and even years for these broken children to understand that they deserve to be treated well; that they deserve love. They are slow to accept the right to expect to be treated with esteem and be regarded with honor by virtue of their birth as human beings. Once this awareness is realized the person begins to live humbly and their confidence soar.

Dr. Viktor Frankl, the distinguished psychiatrist and author of, *Man's Search for Meaning,* had a great impact on my life as I began to think about what I wanted to be, do, become, and have lodged securely in my life. "What you believe you will receive." In other words, what you choose to believe affects how you behave and what you develop that comes in your life. Your attitude most surely affects your altitude.

Dr. Frankl was a Jew imprisoned by the Nazis in the Second World War. His wife, children, and parents were all murdered in the Holocaust. He was made to strip and stand totally naked before his tormentors. They took everything including his wedding band. Yet, he said to himself, "You can take away my wife, you can take away my children, you can strip me of my clothes and my freedom, but there is one thing no person can take away from me—and that is my freedom to choose how I will react to what happens to me." He understood his inalienable right for human dignity and therefore lived confidently in the face of adversity.

Ultimately, Frankl was to say that circumstances do not determine your life; you determine the direction and ultimate culmination of what your life will be. You *can* choose how to respond to what happens to you in your life. You can choose to become bitter or better. You can choose to have life that is like heaven on earth or a living hell. It is up to you.

Jesus said, "Blessed are the poor in spirit and those who are persecuted for what is right for theirs is the kingdom of heaven." In other words, "Blessed are those who have made a conscious estimation of themselves and their circumstances and still choose to do what is right even in the face of persecution and opposition. They will have a taste of heaven on earth before they are in heaven."

When my daughter Sarah was only ten she had already seen more than most children her age. She had held babies so badly abused that they nearly died. She had watched as infants went through withdrawal from heroin, and she had seen children arrive from a murder scene shaken and silent by what they had witnessed. She once said, "Daddy, some people really do experience hell on earth don't they?" After which she said, "I'm sorry for saying hell. Oops, I said it again."

"Yes Darling they do experience a bit of hell. But we're here to let them experience a bit of heaven on earth by showing love and providing a safe place to heal and grow. We are blessed to be a blessing."

LIVE PREPAREDLY

"Those who fail to plan, plan to fail," goes the saying. Liane and I have had to be prepared for anything as the only emergency home for birth to five years in a city of three million. We are on call 365 days a year. We will receive during the course of any given year between 50 and 85 children. These children will remain in our care for a few hours, days, weeks, or years depending on their situation, as we have done for the last 15 years.

Often when we receive a child it will be in the wee hours of the morning. They may come into our home with few physical problems or tragic circumstances. Some may arrive with special food requirements due to their culture or religious background. Others may arrive appearing close to death from starvation. Still other children will have G-Tubes attached to their abdomen or down their nose. A G-tube is a device that is inserted surgically—in many cases—through the stomach wall, directly into the stomach. It remains there for a period of time. At pre-determined intervals, a specially balanced feeding solution is dripped into the tube either by gravity or by pump. Other children will arrive in a near full body cast because of the severity of the abuse. We do our best to have every size of diaper, and different type of formula and every bottle nipple found in stores because we never know what each child will need. And invariably when we have thought we were prepared for anything and have seen it all the phone rings and we are faced with something new. That is the reality of the life we are blessed to receive.

When one is prepared for nearly anything it means that when the unexpected happens it makes it easier to deal with its problems. So everyone should live preparedly.

LIVE RESOLUTELY

"If you stand for nothing you will fall for anything." Be resolute in your beliefs. Know what you value. Hold onto what is true. When you hold tight to those beliefs, values and truths, they will be the anchors that will hold you and steady you in the face of threatened hurricanes, trials, and troubles that inevitably roar into your life.

9

Life Can Be Distressing—Be Comforting

The question I have had asked of me more than any other for more than 20 years is: "Why do bad things happen to good people?" The fact is life is filled with brokenness. That is the reality of life. Bad things happen. Good things happen to bad people, bad things happen to good people, good things happen to good people, bad things happen to bad people. Life's reality. "The rain falls on the just and the unjust," we are told in scripture. When you really think about it why shouldn't bad things happen to good people? We walk on the same sidewalks, buy groceries from the same stores, and live in the same world. Bad things happen. There is no escaping it. Jesus said, "In this world you will have tribulation." There is no way around it.

Perhaps the most frustrating question is, *"What happens to good people when bad things occur?"* We look to the Beatitudes for the answer. The wonderful thing about the scriptures is that they never try to avoid asking the hard questions or facing the ugly realities of life.

The late Alistair Maclean, a young Highland minister who died too early after giving promise of wonderful gifts of mind and heart, tells in his fine book, *High Country*, of two English explorers some time ago who happened onto an Egyptian Tomb. The Tomb was shut by the iron silence of three thousand years. When they opened it they found an exquisitely carved sarcophagus of a little child, and over it this inscription: *"Oh, my life, my love, my little one, would to God I had died for thee!"* After reading it, they walked into the light; then sealed the tomb and left love and death to their eternal vigil.

How old sorrow is. It is common to everyone. I am not thinking of bereavement alone, for though that is so very painful, there are other experiences which make the heart sad and seem, for a time at least, to pull all the sunshine from the sky.

Yet, we are told to find our bliss in brokenness. Jesus said, "Blessed are they that mourn…" Blessed, blissful, contented—in other words—happy are the sad. Now, if that isn't strange, I don't know what is. Yet, if we stop long enough to think about it—if we take the time to ponder on it we will find the truth of it. And in so doing, we can begin to make a bit of sense out of suffering.

Blake saw it this way:

Joy and woe are woven fine
A clothing of the soul divine
Underneath each grief and pine
Runs a joy of silken twine.
When this we rightly know
Safely through the world we go.

Under each grief and pine runs a joy with silken twine. I wonder, perhaps that is part of the problem—we don't get underneath it. We just want to get past it, get away from it, and get beyond it. So we never get underneath it and especially deal with it.

That is why we say such silly things when faced with someone going through their sorrow. When a child's specially loved toy is broken and eyes full of tears, it isn't much good saying—but we do say it—"Don't cry, it doesn't matter, it didn't cost much. You'll get over it. We'll get you another." But it does matter, and everyone who knows and loves children knows that no toy really can replace one that was once loved and now lay broken, or is lost.

Yes, grief is common, but to say so, is to forget that individual hearts do the breaking. Soren Kierkegaard understood this, "It requires moral courage to grieve. It requires religious courage to rejoice." Jesus had the moral courage to grieve, for He wept over Jerusalem and over friends who died. When we act in this moral courage and grieve we understand and acknowledge the tragic dimensions of life. Without it, we are superficial.

When we grasp this, we are on the road to experiencing bliss. We have a choice when life is hard. We can become bitter—or better.

WE BECOME BITTER IN LIFE WHEN WE FORGET THE REALITY OF LIFE

An Arab Proverb says, "All sunshine makes a desert." The trouble-free life is likely to be a shallow life. The truth is we often learn more and mature more from times of sorrow than from times when everything is going well. A familiar poem by Robert Browning Hamilton expresses this truth:

I walked a mile with Pleasure,
She chattered all the way,
But left me none the wiser
For all she had to say

I walked a mile with Sorrow,
And ne'er a word said she,
But, oh, the things I learned from her
When Sorrow walked with me.

To know no grief, is to never to have known love. For grief is an expression of love. It is recognition of love. It is an act of appreciation for the person we have loved. That is why "It is better to have loved and lost then never to have loved at all." And that is why it is always so hard to accept. Yet, read what as the great statesman and philosopher Seneca has said, "The things that were hardest to bear are sweetest to remember."

BLESSINGS AND OBITUARIES

Maybe it is something that comes with age or vocation; but over the last few years I started reading the obituaries. I know that many of you do it as well. Perhaps you've done it to see if someone you know has died. Or to remind you that you are still alive and have at least that for which to be thankful.

Have you noticed that when you read the names—the names and stories of people you don't know—you don't grieve as others do? You may have pity, or sympathy, you may even feel sorry for the family because of a tragedy, but you don't grieve—for you did not know them and so have not grown to love them.

This means that we are blessed when we mourn because we

experience the love expressed in the pain of feeling for those who are lost. It is only because we have had love in our lives that we mourn the loss of it. So it *is* better that we have loved and lost that love than to never have experienced the profound blessing of love in our lives.

10

Life Can Be Dissatisfying—Be Contented

Have you ever awakened in the middle of the night feeling hungry? After going downstairs and opening the fridge have you found yourself standing there wondering what you wanted? So you pick a bit here, and a bit there. You have a bit of this and a bit of that until you felt filled but not quite satisfied.

People find this to be true not only with food, but also in other areas of their lives as well. Many found themselves filling their lives with various things, yet still finding their lives unfulfilled. They are satiated but never satisfied.

Mother Teresa observed during one of her early visits to America after a commercial was shown about weight loss products, "In India people are dying of physical starvation. But in America, people are dying of emotional and spiritual starvation."

Why are so many of us constantly restless in a pursuit of something more? What is it that we are hungry for? What is it that will satisfy us? Where does genuine satisfaction come from? To find the answer to these questions, we must look at the things we use to try to fill that emptiness.

POCKETS, PENNIES AND POSSESSIONS

The first way people have tried to satisfy the hunger within has been through trying to fill their pockets and lives with pennies and possessions. Money and material possessions have largely been, over the years, a measurement of achievement, happiness but all too often providing limited satisfaction.

A billboard for a savings and loans company in Dallas, Texas read, "We lend happiness at eighteen locations." Do they? Society generally believes that if we have enough pennies in our pockets and possessions in our homes we will feel fulfilled. Our newspapers and televisions shout to us that our ultimate fulfillment will be found in their products. And so we fill our homes with more things, often that we could do without.

I remember how, after a good friend died, we set about to help the only relative sort out the things she wanted to keep and arrange to sell the rest at yard sales. It seems strange that after a lifetime of working to earn the money to acquire all of these things, they were sold for pennies on the dollar.

I read of a man who stood to speak at a funeral
of his friend.
He read the dates on his tombstone from the beginning
to the end.
First came the date of his birth. And he read the
following date with tears.

But what mattered most was the dash between
those two years.
For that dash represents all the time upon this earth.
And now only those that knew him and loved him
know what the little line is worth.
For it matters not how much we own,
The car, the house, the cash
What matters most of all in life is how we lived,
and how we loved.
And how we spent that dash.

Isn't that true? Isn't it how we have spent our lives that matters most, not the money we have spent throughout our life.

PLEASURE OF THE SENSES

Most, if not all, don't plan to be multimillionaires, but what we would prefer is that we should have a good time while we are here and living comfortably. The purpose of life, for those who live according to the pleasure of their senses is to enjoy oneself as one moves across the years. So as much as possible, we should avoid pain and stress and pursue those activities that give pleasure.

Now, of course there is nothing wrong with wanting to feel good. It is right and natural that we should want to live in comfortable homes, surrounded by our loved ones. There is nothing wrong with ease and comfort, the trouble comes only when we begin to measure life in such terms; when we make our pleasure the final criterion in how we live.

A husband and wife visited an orphanage where they hoped to adopt a child. In an interview with the boy they wanted, they told him in glowing terms about the many things they could give him. To their amazement, the little fellow said, "If you can only give me a good home, clothes, toys then I might as well stay where I am. I get those things here."

"What then do you want?" asked the mother-to-be.

"I just want someone to love me," was the reply.

Money, material possessions and pleasure can go only so far.

PURSUIT OF POWER

People have tried to satisfy the hunger within them through the pursuit of power. People have tried to fill the emptiness by building little empires.

In *Weekend Magazine* an article on the world's most successful men, stated, "That each are not particularly happy, and that many have noted that each has this in common—a sad face." A famous reporter once asked, "What does it take to make people happy? Money? Fame? Success? Good health? Children? Youth?"

I came across a picture in a book about the Kennedy family. It had young David Kennedy sitting outside the White House. The picture had been taken several years before by his Aunt Jacqueline and was inscribed by his Uncle John with the words, "A future President inspects his property." Though he had name, status, wealth, and all that money could buy, he chose to throw this all away through suicide. Prestige and power are a poor replacement for happiness.

We influence people.

A man by the name James Stanton drove down Victoria Park Avenue and stopped when he reached Queen Street in Toronto with four guns and 6,000 rounds of ammunition ready and willing to kill everyone in sight; until a little dog walked up to him and began to lick his hand. As a result of the kindness of a dog, he decided to flag down a police officer to turn himself in saying the dog and the people were too nice in that neighborhood to kill.

It doesn't take much to make a difference and be a positive influence. If a dog can have such a positive influence just imagine what you can do.

We all influence people. A mother took her young son shopping. After shopping in one store, a clerk handed the little boy a lollipop. "What do you say?" the mother said to the boy, to which he replied, "Charge it!" Parents do influence their children in certain ways. What do you do in your life that one of your parents did? Do you do anything just like they did? Do you have any of their habits?

A TV commercial showed a father walking along with his little boy. The little boy was probably about three years old. The dad picked up a rock and threw it. The boy did the same thing. The father sat down against a tree, lit up a cigarette and laid his pack of cigarettes on the ground. The last scene showed the little boy reaching for that pack of cigarettes. Parents forever influence their children whether they realize it or not! What we do influences others! Sometimes we help to sharpen others and sometimes we drag them down, but we do influence one another! We influence one another in many ways and about many things. If, however, we want to be a positive influence on the lives of those around us there are a few things we can do.

"Blessed or happy are those who hunger and thirst for righteousness they will be satisfied." The righteous person is the person who is in right relationship with God and others. It is the one who has had that relationship with God and others made right.

Chuck Colson understood this. He had had it all as he worked with President Nixon; until he was sent to prison. It was there, after everything—the money, power, position, prestige—were taken away that he came face to face with the one person who could bring the satisfaction that he was searching for through so many other things. It was there that he turned his life over to Christ.

The whole purpose of his life changed after that and he began a ministry to prisoners. His whole purpose and satisfaction changed.

President Ulysses Grant was being taught the game of golf. The man carefully placed the ball on the tee and took a swing. The club hit the turf and scattered dirt all over the president again and again. Finally, the President said, "There seems to be a fair amount of exercise in the game, but what is the purpose of the ball?"

The same could be asked of you. What is the purpose of your life? Saint Francis captured the imagination of the people of his time and all generations because he chose to live with simplicity and grace when in fact he could have lived with wealth and prosperity.

Francis was born in the stony hill town of Assisi in Umbria. His father was a wealthy merchant. He came from wealth yet found no satisfaction within it. He left it all and spent the rest of his days visiting hospitals, especially the refuge for lepers. He spent his life on living on purpose. He lived the prayer that made him famous.

"Lord, make me an instrument of your peace
Where there is hatred, let me bring love.
Where there is injury, let me bring pardon.
Where there is discord, let me bring union.
Where there is doubt, let me bring faith.
Where there is error, let me bring truth
Where there is despair, let me bring hope.
Where there is sadness, let me bring joy.
Where there is darkness, let me bring light.
O Divine Master, grant that I may not so much seek to be consoled as to console, to be understood as to understand, to be loved as to love. For it is in giving that we receive. It is in pardoning that we are pardoned. It is in dying that we are born to eternal life."

St. Francis, and others, have found this to be true and a far better pathway.

11

Life Is Brutal—Be Merciful

Sometimes, you *can* go home again, and it *is* just as you remember it—at least some of it. I returned home to Thunder Bay and attended my church home Current River United. Having spent time with my father in the hospital the days before, and the funeral director the evening before to make the future arrangements for my father; I arrived just as the service was starting and sat on the end of the second last pew on the right, where I had always sat after returning to the church, and until I was invited to join the choir a few months later. Everything was as I had remembered it—even some of the people—though now older and grayer.

I could see myself as a child being hushed by my mother in the fourth pew from the front on the left side. Some have said it didn't work for I'm still talking in church.

Returning, after 22 years, to sit in the pew where it all began—I thought of God's mercy, their mercy and that of others.

As Shakespeare eulogized,

The quality of mercy is not strain'd,
It droppeth as the gentle rain from heaven
Upon the place beneath: it is twice blest;
It blesseth him that gives and him that takes.

We live in a world where it's so easy to become callused and indifferent. We are bombarded daily with news of tragedies, violent acts and suffering people. Living sanely in such a world as this, often necessitates developing a thick skin. Unfortunately, a thick skin and a hard heart are often confused with one another. Instead of developing a thick skin, many develop a hard heart.

THE BRUTALITY OF LIFE WITHOUT MERCY

There is brutality to a life without mercy. Is there not? For the most part, the days in which Jesus lived and taught were not characterized by mercy. A popular Roman philosopher called mercy "The disease of the soul." It was the supreme sign of weakness. Mercy was a sign that you did not have what it takes to be a real man and especially a real Roman. The Romans glorified manly courage, strict justice, firm discipline, and above all, absolute power. They sneered at mercy, because mercy to them was weakness and weakness was despised above all other human limitations.

Though today, we catch a glimpse of mercy every once in a while, we still live in a society where we glory in brutality—our society is fascinated by it. We watch with delight gory movies while getting our fix. And then we watch with righteous disgust the news of countries like Afghanistan, Iraq and others in turmoil.

T. S. Eliot referred to this, when he coined the phrase; "Thunder without rain." Everyone of us, has been outside when we heard thunder in the distance, yet no rain had fallen. Thunder can be a frightening thing. It can seem menacing to a little child in the dark, and even an adult in the light. The crack of thunder can send shivers up and down one's spine.

Eliot, was suggesting that the phrase, signifies the threat from the heavens without any blessing to soften its severity. It is judgment without mercy. It is legalism without liberty.

I once found one of my boys, when he was very young, huddled in a corner of his bed with his legs and knees drawn up to his chin crying. Each time it thundered the tears would stream down from his eyes. His cheeks were burned by the salt from the tears. And through the tears the words came. "Daddy, why doesn't it rain? I like the rain—because if the thunder and lighting start a fire the rain will put it out."

Too much of life is thunder without rain—brutality without mercy. We need to remember to tread softly.

"Blessed are the merciful, for they shall obtain mercy."

THE EQUALITY OF MERCY

Notice not only the brutality to a life without mercy, notice also, the equality of mercy. The law and justice say: "If you do this, this is the punishment you will receive." Physics says: "For every action there is an opposite and equal reaction." Justice also says, "If you do this, this is what you must do to put things right."

Gamaliel, the famous rabbi, is quoted in the Talmud as saying, "Whenever thou hast mercy, God will have mercy on thee." What he said is true. Jesus said, "For if you forgive men for their transgressions, your heavenly Father will also forgive you. But if you do not forgive men, then your Father will not forgive your transgressions" (Matthew 6:14-15 NASB).

James 2:13 reads, "For judgment will be merciless to one who has shown no mercy; mercy triumphs over judgment." When we show no mercy, we are the losers in terms of God's mercy. If we do not show mercy, no mercy will be shown to us.

There were a group of U. S. soldiers living in a rented house in South Korea after the fierce conflict there. They had a houseboy working for them and they would play terrible practical jokes on him. A bucket of water was placed on the top of a slightly ajar door and he would open it and the water would spill getting him wet and making a mess of everything. He would have to clean it up, of course. They would put grease on the knobs on his stove making them slippery. They would dump dirt on the floor or track mud in on their feet. It just went on and on and this little Korean guy would just smile and nod and keep on going whistling a happy tune. One day the GIs could stand it no more and began feeling really bad about their behavior. No matter what they did he just took it and never got angry. It finally got to them. So they decided to go to him and apologize. They told him that they had not treated him well and they were never going to do it again. They really meant business.

He asked, "no more water on top of door?"

They said "no, no more water."

He said, "No more grease on knobs."

They said, "No, no more grease."

He said, "No more dirt in floor?"

"No, no more," they said. The Korean replied with a big happy smile crossing his face: "OK, then I no more spit in soup!" Yes, we give back what we get.

Notice not only the brutality to a life without mercy, and the equality of mercy. Notice finally the quality of mercy. "Blessed are the merciful, for they shall obtain mercy."

The person who is merciful is described as being "kind," or "forgiving," or "people who take pity on others," and "who show mercy to others", and "one who is giving." Merciful is from the Greek that means "charitable and compassionate."

Jesus stated that the people of his kingdom were to be givers, not takers. "Blessed are the merciful, for they shall obtain mercy." "Blessed are the charitable and the compassionate for they will be blessed with that in return."

An elderly man who was new to an area was walking near the seashore, when he saw a young man in the distance running from the shore to the sea and tossing something into the sea he had picked up from the sand. As he approached him, he noticed that he was picking up starfish and tossing them alive into the sea. Each day this same man ran from the shore to the sea tossing starfish. After a few weeks of seeing this, he stopped the man and asked why he was doing it, to which he replied, "Because I can."

"Isn't it pointless to bother, they may only be beached again tomorrow?"

"Then tomorrow I'll be back again. Because, if nothing else, I can be a saver of starfish. I can save this life." As he walked away the man watched the young man continue to toss starfish back into the sea, something seemed to touch his soul again. Perhaps it was only that what seemed pointless before, became a little more important or perhaps the weight of the world seemed to slip away just for a moment, because he knew he could be a starfish saver too—that he could make a difference if only in this small way. And so he found himself stooping, to pick up a starfish and tossing it back into the sea.

Have you ever thought that all we need is encouragement? Encouragement means "to give courage, confidence; to hearten, reassure, bouy up, to exhort." We all need to be reassured or to bouy up every once in awhile. That's because life is hard. And all too often it hurts.

Words can help or hinder. They can either push down or up lift a person.

A young couple had planned on a pleasant day trip. And as can happen, they had a little tiff. However, as tiffs can go, this one grew and grew, until they drove in stony silence. As they passed a field with long haired mules on the field the man said to his wife, "Relatives of yours?"

"Yes," came the response, "on my husband's side."

We laugh because we have been there. All need encouragement, and that is not the way to give it. However, even when were trying, sometimes it doesn't work, so we need to be careful how you give it. Let me give you a few examples:

A women said to a minister; "Pastor, you don't know how much your sermons have meant to my husband since he lost his mind!"

A man said as he left the service, "If I'd of known that you were going to be good today, I'd have brought a friend."

"Well, Pastor, you certainly know how to fill out the time."

"The best one was the one where the minister was speaking at another church. Afterward, when people were leaving a man with flaming red hair came to shake his hand. As he did, he said, "You read your sermon," and then went to the end of the line. When he reached the front again, he said, "And you didn't read it very well." Again he returned to the line, and when he reached him a third time he said." And it wasn't worth reading."

Finally the minister quite upset went to the elders and asked about the man, saying that he was quite rude. They asked, "Did this man have flaming red hair." "Yes," said the minister. In hopes of encouraging him they said, "Don't mind him he just repeats what other people say."

Now, that is brutal.

CHARITY

"Blessed are the merciful, for they shall obtain mercy." Mercy comes from two Greek words, charity and compassion. Charity refers to the old meaning of the word—in the sense of loving concern—making the choice to be kind when others are callous and uncaring. This is a love that "…bears all things, hopes all things, endures all things, a love that never fails."

A man took his wife out on their anniversary to an airport for a flight in a small single engine plane. She had always wanted to feel the wind in her hair. When he got there, he began to argue about the price with the pilot. He wanted one price for the both of them, and the pilot was going to charge them separately for the same flight. Finally, in exasperation, the pilot said, "I'll make a deal with you. If you can take this flight and not make a sound then, afterward I'll give you all your money back. If you make any sound, you will owe me the full price." The man made the deal and he and his wife climbed in and off they went. Now, you know what the pilot did. He made flips and dives and turns to try to make the man cry out. But not a sound. After landing, the pilot said, "Well, I must say you surprised me. Here is your money back, I thought you would have made a sound."

"Well," said the man, "I almost did."

"When?" asked the pilot.

"When my wife fell out."

This man did love something, but it was the wrong thing.

COMPASSION

"Blessed are the merciful, for they shall obtain mercy." Mercy not only means charity, but also, compassion.

To have compassion means to show someone kindness and grace. Grace as we know refers to God's action towards us in Christ and our action towards others because of Christ. As the acronym GRACE explains it fully: it is God's Riches At Christ's Expense.

Compassion, grace, or mercy means loving and caring for someone without the person deserving it, and even times when the person doesn't deserve it, because we ourselves have been loved, encouraged, cared for, and forgiven in spite of ourselves, by Christ.

A little girl used to be yelled at by her neighbor every time she stepped foot on his lawn and scowled at every time she passed his property. He spent hours grooming the lawn, carefully tending and weeding. One day, he was not out as usual and the little girl asked why. Her mother said that his wife had died. Later that day, the little girl watched as the man just sat on the porch. She sheepishly walked over to the old curmudgeon being careful not to step on his lawn and climbed up in his lap and gave him a hug.

Later she returned home. Her mother asked what she had been doing. She told her that she was over at Mr. Jones. Shocked, she asked, "What were you doing there?" The little girl said, "I just sat with him and cried."

Dante Gabriel Rossetti, the famous 19th century poet and artist, was once approached by an elderly man. The old fellow had sketches and drawings that he wanted Rossetti to look at and tell him if they were any good, or if they at least showed potential talent.

Rossetti looked them over carefully. After the first few he knew that they were worthless. But Rossetti was a kind man, and he told the elderly man as gently as possible that the pictures were without much value. The visitor was disappointed, but seemed to expect Rossetti's judgement. He then apologized for taking up Rossetti's time, but would he just look at a few more drawings—these created by a young student?

Rossetti looked over the second batch of sketches and immediately became enthusiastic over the talent they revealed. "These," he said, "oh, these are good. This young student has great talent. He should be given every help and encouragement in his career as an artist. He has a great future if he will work hard and stick it out." Rossetti could see that the old fellow was deeply moved. Who is this fine young artist?" he asked. "Your son?"

"No", said the man sadly. "It is me—40 years ago. If only I had heard your praise then! For you see, I got discouraged and gave up—too soon."

At times, we also become discouraged and want to give up and if only someone came to have compassion on us and offer encouragement.

Let me encourage you. You're not alone. Sometimes you think you are. And you think that no one in the world understands what you are going through. But you're wrong. You're very wrong.

12

Life Is Frantic— Be the One to Design a Sanctuary of Serenity

A noted British preacher, J. H. Jowett, believed that inner peace comes not from tranquil circumstances but from an untroubled heart. "If we were to hear 100 people repeat the scripture, 'Let not your heart be troubled,' we should find that 99 will put the emphasis upon the word *troubled*...I feel led to believe that the purposed emphasis is on the word *heart*... The heart is to be clothed in serene regality even when hell is knocking and rioting at its very gates." In other words, "We are to have an untroubled heart."

We have had to face hardships, at some point within our lives. The dictionary shows "trial, burden, or privation, the thwarting of hope." Yet, none of us needs a dictionary to tell us about hardship and frustration. We live with it. The ambitious dreams that are never quite realized; the door of opportunity that is suddenly slammed shut, the separation or divorce that destroys our dreams; some hardships are large others are small.

However, every one of us has to contend with them. The way in which we deal with them determines, in large measure, the success or dissatisfaction of our lives.

Everyone has, at some point, said or thought, "Why?" "Why have my plans for a happy life, marriage, business, or future retirement been blocked? Why doesn't anything work out as I want it too?" At some point in our lives most of us have these questions, in one form or another.

DESIGN A SANCTUARY OF SERENITY

When facing the turbulence of life we must design a sanctuary of serenity. We do this when we face life realistically. Many people refuse to take a clear, comprehensive and realistic look at their life and at life in general. The reality of life is that there could be hard times ahead. It may not have happened yet to you. Or you may already be in the midst of it; or you may have just come through it and are standing surveying the shattered landscape of your life. Wherever you are right now, you need to take a clear, comprehensive and realistic look at your surroundings. Don't avoid it. Don't deny the need to do it. Don't run away from it. Just face it.

To design a sanctuary of serenity you must take a clear look at the landscape of your life. Remember, "If you fail to plan you're planning to fail" When you truly comprehend that just like a weight room in a gym has machines to develop muscle and cause pain; life too has trials built into it to develop and enlarge you, emotionally, psychologically, physically, and spiritually. When you understand this you will start to plan for it. Just as a business has a contingency fund put aside for unforeseen problems or opportunities; and just as some people save for a rainy day, so you must build your sanctuary of serenity on the foundation of reality.

Dr. Leslie Weatherhead understood this. A few years ago, considered to be one of the greatest communicators in the world, as well as a distinguished psychologist, in middle-age he entered a period of depression that was so very deep it threatened to overtake him. He remembers during this shattering time holding on to a quotation of Browning's *Paracelsus*.

If I stoop into a dark tremendous sea of cloud
It is but for a time.
I hold God's lamp close to my breast.
Its splendor soon or late will pierce the gloom
I shall emerge one day.

In the darkest night of his life the sentence that he held onto was, "I shall emerge one day." He knew that God's lamp—His Word—was a lamp unto his feet, and a light unto his way. He knew he would be guided through the storm-tossed sea of depression. He had built into his life a sanctuary of serenity. He knew where to turn when he was having troubles that he couldn't cope. He didn't avoid the reality of problems. He didn't say that just because he had helped hundreds of thousands of people with his books and lectures that he himself was immune to the realities of sorrow, struggle, depression or despair. He had understood that this comes to all of us from which he would emerge one day.

Do you remember Miss Havisham in *Great Expectations*? Dickens describes her as the woman who had ruined her life because she refused to face heartbreak. As a young woman, she had been swept off her feet by a scoundrel. Marriage plans were made. The day set, the dresses bought, the wedding feast prepared. Then, at twenty minutes to nine on the morning of the wedding, the bridegroom's letter comes, canceling the marriage. But she refuses to face it. From that moment on all time stopped. All clocks in the house were stopped, the drapes were drawn. And the food left in its place to rot and spider webs grew over everything.

Dickens is giving us a parable about people's lives. Often, it is much easier to run from hardship than to refuse to face it. But the fact is, we will never find freedom from it until we face it. Certainly, that is the first step in dealing with hardships—and moving from panic to praise. If things aren't working out according to the way we mapped them, change the map.

Reinhold Niebuhr said, "God grant me the serenity to accept the things I cannot change, the courage to change the things I can, and the wisdom to know the difference." Life is filled with things we can't change. That is the reality. Trying to change them will only make you crazy. However, seeking the wisdom to know what you can change and then setting out to change those things will give you courage and confidence.

DISAPPOINTMENTS CAN BE AVENUES FOR NEW DISCOVERIES

When building a sanctuary of serenity you must live life realistically and also creatively. Disappointments can be avenues for new discoveries. Detours can produce a new direction in your life.

We live in a frustrating world. We live in a world that is less than ideal. We need to understand this. And this is not going to change any day soon. But Gandhi said, "Be the change you want to see in the world." Your attitude toward what has happened can change the future. You can be the change you want to see in the world. The frustration I had over the lack of enforcement of the rights and protection of children has not only caused me to open my home to hundreds of children, but to start a small organization that seeks to elevate some of the pain these children go through and advocate for change in our social justice system. My small organization called Compassion@Work has become the avenue of advocacy for child protection. I have become the change I want to see in the world. You can too. Compassion@ Work was created out of the tears shed on my shoulder by children burned by cigarettes and broken by parents who should have loved, nourished and protected them. I wept with them and wondered how best to be the change I wanted to see in the world. The tears on my shoulders reminded me to be the someone who would have something to say. That someone turned out to be me. What about you? What is shouting at you to be that someone, to do or provide that something, to change the world? Encourage others to do the same.

Building a sanctuary of serenity begins when life is lived realistically and continues as it is lived creatively. You too can be the change you want to see in the world.

I was watching the television program *Dateline* as the parents of the girl who had been called the Christian Martyr of Columbine School spoke of writing their book about her life. It tells the true life story of this girl, and how she was not a saint but a girl who was going down the same road as the two boys who killed all those in the massacre at Columbine. Her parents spoke of how she too had wanted to kill them and others and then herself. They spoke of her involvement in Satanism and that it was leading to her suicide. They spoke of how they wanted to bring some good out of this terrible tragedy that had happened in their life and many other families. They wrote the book to hopefully help other parents and children not to go down the same path.

C.S. Lewis did the same a few years ago in his book, *Grief Observed.* He had struggle with the death of his wife. He wrote about the struggle he had with God and his struggles with the meaning of life and then in the end found that as he rested in God, it was there that he found the peace he was looking for.

Building a sanctuary also involves living life *providentially.* A friend asked Martin Luther, "When everybody turns against you, where will you be?" Luther replied, "Right where I am now, in the hands of Almighty God."

There was a young man studying for the ministry. He fell dangerously ill for over a year. At the time of the illness it seemed to be nothing but an inconvenient interruption of his life. He wondered why God would frustrate the plans he had set out for himself, especially when he was doing it for God in the first place. After many years in the ministry, the period of illness was recognized for what it really was—a valuable part of his preparation for pastoral ministry.

The purpose of God is not always made plain from day to day. Things often happen which seem to have no point whatever and that contribute nothing to the total sum of life. However, when we let go and let God we discover that we find peace because we have built a sanctuary of serenity.

PEACE IN SPITE OF PROBLEMS

When Ann Landers was writing her column she received around 10,000 letters a month from people requesting advice on various topics. When asked what her most common question was, she answered that people seem to be afraid or worried about something. They're afraid of losing their health, they worry about their job, and they're filled with concerns about their family. People are fearful about their neighbors or frustrated with their friends. A large number of the letters describe relationships that were nearly ruptured and family fighting. In short, people were looking for peace but couldn't find it. I read an incredible story about a father who was so stressed that he punched out Cookie Monster! Here's the story as it appeared in the online version of USA Today.

A man's plan to have his young daughter meet the Cookie Monster crumbled when he was arrested for allegedly assaulting the furry blue Sesame Street character. Police say Lee P. McPhatter, upset that the Cookie Monster would not pose for a picture at the Sesame Place theme park, shoved and kicked the employee inside the costume. Middletown police said that 21-year-old Jennie McNelis suffered bruised ribs and a cervical sprain when McPhatter shoved her to the ground, then kicked her in the head and back. McPhatter said he would fight the charges, which include simple assault, harassment and disorderly conduct.

Peace is regarded as one of the primary virtues that people crave, and yet it is so often absent from lives today. From "Road Rage" to "Cookie Conflicts," to "Disney Disasters" our culture does not behave peacefully.

We long for it, we desire it, we crave it, but we seldom find it.

The reason is because we need peace *with* God. It was St. Augustine that said, "We are restless until we rest in Thee O God." He has proven over and over to be right.

We are a world filled with worries; a race ravaged by fears. We are a people without peace, living in an age of anxiety, worry, and fear.

The story is told of a man who conned his way into the orchestra of the emperor of China many years ago although he could not play a note. Whenever the group practiced or performed, he would hold his flute against his lips, pretending to play but not making a sound. He received a modest salary and enjoyed a comfortable living. On the day the emperor requested a solo from each musician, the flutist became extremely nervous. There wasn't enough time to learn the instrument. He pretended to be sick, but the royal physician wasn't fooled. On the day of his solo performance, the impostor took poison and killed himself. The explanation of his suicide led to a phrase that found its way into the English language; "He refused to face the music."

Dr. George Crane of Chicago was speaking to a judge one day about people with mental disorders. The judge asked if it were true that people today have more mental disorders than in the past. Dr. Crane stated that there were definitely more today.

The judge then asked, "What then would be the best way to eliminate the problems?"

Dr. Crane stated, "There would be much less strain on men and women if they teamed up with God. People try to ignore God and are soon overwhelmed with innumerable fears and worries."

We need peace with God, and to make peace *for* God. "Blessed are the peacemakers for they shall be called the children of God."

Approximately 110 years later, President Ronald Reagan dubbed the new mobile M-X missile "The Peacekeeper." It is interesting that both references refer to weapons. In fact, if you make an internet search with the word "peacekeeper," most of the references are to weapons, soldiers, and wars.

It seems that today if someone is going to try to "keep the peace," that person will need to have the ability to enforce it. That often means weapons, sometimes the more the better. It appears that peacekeeping is at best, a temporary solution that is ladened with danger and difficulty.

History has shown that most peacekeeping efforts have had only mixed results and often the peacekeepers are shot. Did you know that in the over 3100 years of recorded world history, the world has only been at peace 8% of the time? That means that the world has experienced only a total of 286 years of peace. During that time 8000 treaties have been made and broken.[26]

In 1968 a major newspaper reported that there had been 14,553 known wars from 36 BC to date. Since 1945 there have been over 70 wars and more than 200 significant outbreaks of violence. From 1958 over 100 nations have been involved in one way or another in armed conflict.[27]

What most people do not seem to understand is that peace is not something that can be imposed from the outside. You cannot "keep" a peace that isn't there.

John MacArthur says, "A truce just says you don't shoot for awhile. Peace comes when the truth is known, the issue is settled, and the parties embrace each other."This is the reason that Jesus, in this verse, did not use the word, "peacekeeper," he used the word, "peacemaker." There is a world of difference. A peacekeeper is a person who tries to enforce the peace by whatever means necessary. That may be by force of personality or by superior weapons, or a truce.

A peacemaker is one who actually discovers the origin of the conflict, and finds a way to resolve it, and helps the parties to restore a proper, loving relationship.

As believers, that is what we are to be doing and being. We

are to be about making peace and being peacemakers.

We need peace with God, and then we can make peace for God, and finally, receive the peace *of* God.

In 1871 the city of Chicago was nearly destroyed by fire. This was known as the Great Chicago Fire. Over 300 people died during the fire and approximately 100,000 were left homeless.

One of the heroes of the Great Chicago Fire was Horatio Gates Spafford. Spafford was an attorney during this time. He had lost a great deal of real-estate in the fire. Despite such great personal financial loss and then combined with the untimely death of his son (during this same time period) Spafford for two years unselfishly helped to assist the needs of the homeless, impoverished, and grief-stricken caused by the fire. Such merciful and kind acts as these to his fellow-men just helped to strengthen the testimony as to why Horatio G. Spafford was known throughout Chicago as a sincere, devout Christian.

After two years of such work, in November 1873 Spafford and his family decided to take a vacation. Because Spafford was a loyal friend and supporter of Dwight L. Moody, he and his family decided that they would meet with Moody and Ira Sankey on one of their evangelistic campaigns in England, and from there the Spaffords planned to travel on to Europe. Just as the Spafford's were preparing to leave, Horatio was unexpectedly detained by urgent business concerns in Chicago. The decision was made that his wife Anna and their daughters, Anna (Annie), Maggie, Bessie, and Tanetta would continue on as scheduled to England. Once after Spafford had resolved the business concern he would then catch up with them on the other side of the Atlantic Ocean.

The ship, the S.S. Ville du Harve, on which his wife and daughters were traveling never reached England. Off Newfoundland, the ship collided with an English sailing vessel, the Loch Earn. The ship sank within 20 minutes after it was struck. Mrs. Spafford was only one of the 47 to survive; tragically all four of their daughters were part of the 226 who perished in the aftermath. Anna Spafford's heartbreaking telegram to her husband simply read: "Saved alone."Horatio immediately set sail for England to join his grief-stricken wife. As the ship that he was traveling on passed the approximate location where his daughters had drowned, (it is reported) that due to his deep sorrow mingled with his unwavering faith in God's goodness that he penned the words of his now famous hymn—"It Is Well with My Soul."

When peace like a river attendeth my way,
When sorrows like sea-billows roll,
Whatever my lot, Thou has taught me to know;
"It is well, it is well with my soul."

BEING THE CHANGE YOU WANT TO SEE IN THE WORLD

In an age of relativism the real rebels are those who hold to the truth that virtue matters. If you truly desired to learn to be human in this inhumane world; you will sow seeds of wisdom, justice, courage, self-discipline, faith, hope, love, righteousness, mercy, peace and comfort into your life and the lives around you. By doing so you will be the change you want to see in the world.

The real rebels are not those who seek to thwart the rule of law and overthrow governments but who seek justice, love, mercy and walk humbly with their God and all humanity. By doing so, they create a better world and become truly humane human beings.

NOTES

1 www.newadvent.org/cathen/15472a.htm
2 William A. Ulmer, *The Christian Wordsworth*, 1798-1805 (Albany: State University of New York Press, 2001), p152.
3 Thomas Aquinas, *Basic Writings of St. Thomas Aquinas*, vol. 2, ed. Anton C. Pegis (Indianapolis, IN: Hackett, 1997), Summa, Q 61, art. 5, p.473
4 Bible Philippians 4:8
5 Dave Pelzer, *A Child Called It*, Health Communications Inc. Deerfield Beach, Florida, 1993 p. 55
6 Ibid., p. 48
7 Ibid., p.65
8 Ibid., p.62
9 *National Post*, Tuesday April 5, 2005, "8-year-old boy youngest ever to hang himself" p. A10
10 Ibid.
11 Thomas Aquinas, *Summa Theologica*, IIa-IIae, quest. 123, art 2, p. 197
12 Aristotle, *Nicomachean Ethics*, II 3, 1105a32; Cicero, Rhetoric, De Inventione, II 54.

13 Stephen R. Covey, *The Seven Habits of Highly Effective Families*, Franklin Covey-Golden Books N.Y. 1977, p.17

14 Dick DeVos, *Rediscovering American Values*, Plume Publishing, 1997, pp.202-203

15 Bible James 1:1-4

16 Psalm 41

17 Proverbs 17:5

18 James 1:15-16

19 Jim Wallis, *Faith Works*, Random House New York 2000, p.xxiv

20 Jim Wallis, *Faith Works*, Random House New York, 2000, pg XXIX-XXX.

21 Frank Minirth, *In Pursuit of Happiness*, published by Fleming H. Revell, 2004, p.155-156

22 *Chicken Soup for the Soul*

23 James Dobson, *Hide or Seek*, p.9-10.

24 Scripture John 10:10b

25 Galatians 5:22-23

26 http://www.christianlibrary.org/authors/Grady_Scott/matt5-9.htm

27 http://www.bereanbiblechurch.org/transcripts/som/5_9.htm

ACKNOWLEDGEMENTS

I would like to thank numerous people: first my wife Liane who always encourages me in every new endeavor; our dear friends Rev. Steve and Lynn Davis, your friendship means more than you know, to my mentor and friend Dr. Jim Wetherall who always has a wise and witty word at the right time—thank you all.

I would also like to express my appreciation to the Empire Club of Canada, its Past Presidents and directors who honored Liane and me with the Empire Club of Canada's first humanitarian "Community Service Award."

The church families I have served as minister over the last twenty years, first as a neophyte student minister at Current River United in Thunder Bay, and the Carmen Pastoral Charge in Carmen Manitoba; then as a newly-ordained minister at the Matilda Pastoral Charge near Ottawa, Victoria Park United in Toronto and to St. Andrews United in Markham. You will never know how grateful I am to all for what I have learned from you and with you. It has been such privilege to serve in each pastorate.

And for Karen Petherick's creative work at Intuitive Design International Ltd. Her inspired work speaks for itself when you hold this book in your hands.

And to my publisher, editor, writing mentor and friend Bill Belfontaine; thank you for the many hours of editing, and advice. Thank you for believing in me as an author. You are truly the White Knight with your publishing company.

Bill Belfontaine

When a book with the title *Sacred Parenting, No Ordinary Moments* uses the quote from Barth, "Courage is fear that has said its prayers," you know you are in for a worthwhile read.

Being raised by a TV is not parenting but an abdication of duty that leaves children and youth, in most cases, unprepared for the *real* world that they must live in at home, at school, and as adults.

Is anyone worried about the teaching of respect and love? John Niles is, and you'll see it throughout these pages.

As a publisher of non-fiction books that dwell on issues including Social Concern, we bring to readers, John Niles' comments hoping that change is possible *if* we choose to make something of it.

As one of the leading-edge clergy, and a very well respected advocate for children, he has written again of his experiences with young children and teenagers. His first book, *How I Became Father to 1,000 Children and the Lessons I Learned* clearly laid out how the problem of child abuse festers into unsafe streets and unruly gangs.

The author is a recipient of the Governor General's Award for Meritorius Service, President of the Empire Club of Toronto, a nominee for The Order of Canada and also The Order of Ontario, both well-earned.

ABOUT THE AUTHOR

Dr. John S. Niles

Dr John S. Niles has been in the caring profession for over twenty years; beginning as a graduate in social work specializing with emotionally disturbed children and teens. Later, he provided badly needed service as a counselor and supervisor within the prison system. He later worked in hospital chaplaincy and with the criminally insane in a maximum security prison. Presently, he is the rector of St. Andrew's United Church in Toronto, where he and his wife open their home to infants and young children as the primary emergency home. Together, with their five children, Liane and John have cared for well over 1000 "crack cocaine" and heroin addicted, abandoned and abused children, and the most tragic of those who will never lose their affliction brought on by their mother's alcoholism.

Liane and John Niles received the Governor General's Meritorious Service Medal, the Community Service Humanitarian of the Year award from the Empire Club of Canada in 2000, and the Heart and Spirit Humanitarian of the Year award from the Children's Aid Society of Ontario and have been nominated for the Order of Ontario, and the Order of Canada. He had written as a columnist for *Fellowship Magazine* and articles for the *United Church Observer* and he and his wife have had articles written about their work in the *Faith Today, United Church Observer, Toronto Star*, and *Toronto Sun*, the *Globe*, the *Markham Economist and Sun* as well as being interviewed on *CityTV, CTV* and *On the Line* program for *CTS* as well as local public television and *CBC Radio.*

OTHER WHITE KNIGHT BOOKS

Adoption	A Swim Against The Tide, *David R.I. McKinstry*
Biography	The Life and Times of Nancy Ford-Inman, *Nancy Erb Ke*
Education	From Student to Citizen, *Prof. Peter Hennessy*
Health	Prescription for Patience, *Dr. Kevin J Leonard* Brain Injury, *Alan J. Cooper*
Humor	*By David R.I. McKinstry:* • An Innkeeper's Discretion BOOK ONE • An Innkeeper's Discretion BOOK TWO Will That Be Cash or 'Cuffs?, *Yvonne Blackwood*
Inspiration	"Oh My God. It's ME!", *Dr. Sheryl Valentine* *By Rev. Dr. John S. Niles:* • The Art of Sacred Parenting • How I Became Father to 1000 Children *By Darlene Montgomery:* • Conscious Women, Conscious Lives ONE • Conscious Women, Conscious Lives TWO • Conscious Women, Conscious Careers Happiness: Use It or Lose It, *Rev. Dr. David "Doc" Loomis* Sharing MS (Multiple Sclerosis), *Linda Ironside* Sue Kenney's My Camino, *Sue Kenney*
Personal Finances	Spent Smarter, Save Bigger, *Margot Bai* Don't Borrow $Money$, *Paul E Counter*
Poetry	Loveplay, *Joe Fromstein and Linda Stitt* Two Voices, A Circle of Love, *Serena Williamson Andrew*
Politics & History	*Islam, Women and the Challenges of Today,* Farzana Hassan Prophets of Violence, Prophets of Peace, *Dr. K. Sohail* Turning Points, *Ray Argyle*
Reference	Self-Publishing, *Bill Hushion, Peter Wright* The Complete Guide to Becoming A Firefighter, *Kory Pe*
Self-Help	*By Dr. K. Sohail* • The Art of Living in Your Green Zone • The Art of Loving in Your Green Zone, • The Art of Working in Your Green Zone, *with Bette Da* • Love, Sex and Marriage, *with Bette Davis*
True Crime – Police	"10-45" Spells Death, *Kathy McCormack Carter* Life on Homicide, *Former Police Chief Bill McCormack* The Myth of The Chosen One, *Dr. K. Sohail*

Visit our website www.whiteknightbooks.ca or request catalogue.

RECOMMENDED READING FROM OTHER PUBLISHERS

History	An Amicable Friendship (Canadiana), *Jan Th. J. Krijff* Pro Deo, *Prof. Ronald Morton Smith*
Religion	From Islam to Secular Humanism, *Dr. K. Sohail*
Biography	Gabriel's Dragon, *Arch Priest Fr. Antony Gabriel*